CUSICK

CHAMPION WITHOUT CAUSE

Based on a true story

PHILIP AMORTILA

This book is based on a true story.

It follows boxer Johnny Cusick's rise and fall in the 1930s as narrated by his coach and manager John Bennett. It blends real and fictional elements for narrative ends, with some names and details changed for privacy purposes.

To my dear wife, Lynda

Thank you for sharing your grandfather's story, which forms the foundation of this book. Your inspiration, passion, and support have been invaluable. Without you, this book wouldn't exist.

CONTENT

'Glory is fleeting, but obscurity is forever.'

Napoleon Bonaparte

PROLOGUE

Every so often, fate serves an enigma that challenges our perceptions of passion, ambition, and destiny. Johnny 'Nipper' Cusick was one such puzzle, stitched together by contradictions that defied the conventional wisdom of what drives a person to greatness.

As a youngster in Hulme during the 1930s, Johnny learned the hard way. He was brought up on the Bloodtubs of Manchester—little wooden huts full of screaming fight fans and fought it out in the ring for a few pennies, just enough to buy some fish and chips.

He started fighting at twelve on the streets of All Saints, taking part in fifteen-rounders in the Bloodtubs at fifteen, and turned professional at sixteen, in the summer of 1934.

Over fifteen years, as his coach and manager, I witnessed a mesmerizing dance of strength and vulnerability. Here was a man who stood atop the echelons of British boxing, garnished with the prestigious Lonsdale Belt, the oldest championship belt in British professional boxing—yet harboured an unsettling ambivalence for the very sport that hoisted him into stardom.

Johnny's journey is more than a tale of punches and uppercuts. It's an exploration of an inner landscape marked by conflict, resilience, and the quest for identity in a world rife with expectations. It delves into the potential we unlock when we're compelled into spaces that allow our skills to shine, but in which our hearts may not fully reside.

Cusick's story serves as a beacon. It beckons to all who have grappled with the delicate balance between external achievement and inner fulfilment. And it dares to ask the question: how does one reconcile a world in which you excel at something you never ardently desired?

1

THE BATTLE AGAINST

HUNGER

In the summer of 1934, Manchester pulsed with the frenetic energy of boxing. In and around the city, licensed arenas officially sanctioned by the British Boxing Board of Control played host to the orchestrated dance of the fighters, while in the dark underbelly of the same city, unlicensed venues lurked like grim spectres, squalid backdrops to brutal contests. These were places where the violent ballet of unregulated fights played out in a haze of grit and grime.

In this fervent atmosphere, my footsteps carved a well-trodden path through the streets, drawn by an insatiable hunger for the sport. Every night, and even on Sundays, I was consumed by the fervour of the bouts. In the quiet pre-dawn hours, before the world had fully roused from its slumber, I was already in motion, travelling as far as Birmingham. This wasn't a mere duty, but an unyielding passion—a fire that had ignited four decades prior and blazed on, untamed by the passage of time.

As I stand at the threshold of this narrative, the flame within me still burns as fiercely as it did during those early mornings in 1934. The world may have evolved, but my passion for the sport endures.

At this period, whispers swirled around a young lad—a mere sixteen years old—boxing as often as twice a week. Against all odds, he emerged victorious time and again, defeating his adversaries with a relentless zeal. Yet, it wasn't just his impressive record that piqued my interest—it was an incident.

The boy faced off against a contender named Nipper Mack, a local talent from Manchester. The clash took place in one of those unlicensed places. They duelled for fifteen gruelling two-minute rounds, a marathon of exertion and willpower that left them both teetering on the edge of exhaustion.

In the end, as the crowd held its collective breath, the referee's decision echoed through the clamour: Nipper Mack was declared the victor. But victory came at a cost that would sear itself into my memory—the young opponent crumpled in the ring, his body surrendering to a lifeless faint.

A doctor was summoned. The diagnosis was as unexpected as it was alarming: malnutrition. A battle waged in the heart of the ring, yet it was the battle against hunger that the boy had ultimately lost.

I hadn't been present to witness this event first-hand, but when the tale reached my ears, a spark ignited within me. The sheer audacity of a fighter enduring fifteen rounds under such dire conditions was a testament to his resilience and fortitude.

I dug into inquiries, got hold of the kid's home address, and made up my mind to swing by and talk to his folks. With doubts nagging at me about how they'd take to my visit, I decided to bring along a friend, Mr. Jack Curphey, a well-known name in the boxing scene feeling that his advice could be helpful if things got tricky.

We arrived at the given address, fortunate to find Mr. Cusick at home. Without any preamble I cut straight to the chase.

'Mr. Cusick,' I began, my voice carrying a mix of enthusiasm and earnestness, 'I've seen your son's potential in the ring, and I'm here because I genuinely believe I can help shape his path.'

Mr. Cusick's eyes narrowed thoughtfully, a spark of interest lighting up his gaze. He leaned forward, his voice low and tinged with intrigue. 'Well, at the moment, Johnny's training under Mr. Cahan,' he confided. 'But between you and me, neither of us is too thrilled about it.'

I sensed an opening and leaned in closer. 'So, you think there's a chance Johnny might be open to a change?'

He chuckled softly, a wry smile playing on his lips. 'Let's just say, pulling Johnny away from Cahan's hold won't require moving mountains.'

I wasted no time in tracking down Mr. Cahan, steering my way to the gym whose address had been provided. There, amidst the staccato rhythm of punching bags and the grunts of aspiring fighters, we found him—shaping young athletes, moulding their raw talent. I plunged directly into the matter at hand, and Cahan, to his credit, reciprocated with surprising candour.

He unveiled a less rosy picture of Johnny, filling in gaps that Mr. Cusick had conveniently left blank. 'He's a firecracker, that one,' Cahan admitted, his eyes showing a blend of frustration and resignation. 'More trouble than he's worth right now.'

As we talked, it became increasingly clear that he wouldn't lose much sleep severing ties with Johnny. His contract, once a golden ticket, had lost its lustre. Johnny had recently found himself on the wrong side of the law, stripped of his boxing license by the Board of Control for participating in unsanctioned bouts. The contract was now essentially worthless, a deadweight both parties seemed eager to discard.

Just as Cahan and I were deep in conversation, the gym doors creaked open and in walked Johnny Cusick. I later discovered it was no coincidence—his father had sent him to find me. Seizing the opportunity, I asked Cahan if I could watch the young Johnny in action. He nodded, gesturing toward the ring.

The first sight of Johnny clad in his boxing attire is a moment forever etched in my memory. Here was a young man, slight and seemingly fragile, a stark contrast to the battle-hardened reputation that preceded him. The dissonance was palpable, how could this ethereal figure, almost bird-like in his frailty, have already weathered over a hundred gruelling fights? It was a riddle that hinted at an inner steel far beyond his years.

Johnny stepped into the ring, squaring off against a couple of young hopefuls, and what unfolded before us was nothing short of riveting. The agility, the finesse—he was a revelation. Beside me, Jack Curphey nodded, his eyes widening. It was evident he shared my sense of awe.

Compelled by what I had just witnessed, I knew I had to act swiftly. Pulling Mr. Cahan aside from the spectacle in the ring, I got straight to the point. 'What's your asking price for Johnny's contract?'.

Cahan raised an eyebrow, intrigued, and threw the ball back into my court. 'Make me an offer' he challenged.

Without hesitation, I proposed, 'Five pounds upfront, and another five when—no, if—the Board reinstates Johnny's license.'

Cahan's agreement came swifter than I had expected, as if he'd been waiting for just such an opportunity. We promptly summoned Johnny over, who seemed more than agreeable to the change in stewardship. With a few exchanges—handshakes sealing fates and altering trajectories—we finalized the deal right then and there, cementing a partnership that promised to be as unpredictable as it was exhilarating.

I couldn't wait to share the news, so Johnny and I immediately headed back to his father's place. The atmosphere was charged with expectation as I laid out my ambitious plans for Johnny's future in the ring. Mr. Cusick listened intently, and we reached a momentous agreement: Johnny would move in with me, effectively inaugurating a partnership that would span nearly a decade and a half.

For fifteen years, our lives were a tapestry of triumphs and setbacks, jubilant celebrations and sobering disappointments. It was a complex but enriching chapter that neither of us would ever forget.

In the early days, from the moment Johnny stepped into the ring for his first amateur match in Manchester, everyone noticed something different about him. He might have been small and wiry, but there was more to him than mere size. Johnny possessed an uncanny ability to glide around his opponents with a grace and fluidity that bordered on the otherworldly.

Johnny's footwork was a marvel to behold, reminiscent of a ballet dancer on a stage. He glided, almost floated, his feet barely making a sound as they brushed the ground.

However, what truly earned him the nickname 'Nipper' was an incident that took place during a crucial match early in his career. He was up against a formidable, more experienced opponent, and the crowd had already counted him out. In the third round, just as he was cornered and it seemed like the fight was all but over, Johnny executed a stunning series of moves. He bobbed and weaved, ducking under a fierce hook and emerging unscathed, much like a nipper skilfully evading capture.

The crowd erupted in thunderous cheers, and in that electric moment, Johnny ceased to be just Johnny Cusick he became Johnny 'Nipper' Cusick.

The nickname 'Nipper' captured not only his small and youthful appearance but also his agile fighting style and ability to nip away from danger, to slip through the tightest of spots unscathed. Like a nimble street urchin navigating the bustling streets of Manchester, Johnny 'Nipper' Cusick continued to dazzle the world of boxing, defying expectations and leaving audiences spellbound with his every move.

2

THE ASCENT TO GLORY

The initial task at hand was unequivocal: to sculpt Johnny into a formidable figure, enhancing not only his physical prowess but also his endurance, in preparation for his grand public debut.

Surprisingly, he assimilated into our fold with remarkable ease, almost as if he had always been a part of our family. We embarked on a meticulously crafted regimen, dedicating four evenings each week to meticulously hone his raw talent into something truly extraordinary.

Simultaneously, a close friend of mine arranged a low-key job for Johnny at a mechanic's garage attached to a small petrol station at the outskirts of town. This wasn't glamorous work; the station was in a poor state, and the scent of oil and petrol seemed permanently etched into the air.

However, it offered Johnny more than just a paycheck. The job kept him mentally occupied, and it allowed me to keep a watchful eye. It provided a grounding experience, humbling him to the struggles of daily labour and the intricacy of machinery. While far removed from the boxing rings and athletic showmanship, this garage job served as a parallel training ground, teaching him the values of grit, discipline, and hard work.

For approximately six months, this became our established routine. Fuelled by a disciplined training and nourishing diet, Johnny's transformation was nothing short of remarkable.

Feeling the profound shift in Johnny's disposition and abilities, I sensed it was time to escalate our ambitions. No longer the raw, untested youth he once was, Johnny had evolved into a formidable talent. My next hurdle was to try and restore his boxing license.

I was increasingly convinced that we had a rock-solid endeavour on our hands. If Johnny remained committed, there was no ceiling to what we could achieve as a duo.

Fortified by this belief, I penned a formal letter to the Board, petitioning for Johnny Cusick's reinstatement.

Luck—or perhaps fate—was on my side. At this pivotal moment, I had an invaluable ally on the Board: Mr. Jack Smith, who had an even broader understanding of Johnny's backstory than I did. His influence could tip the scales in our favour, making this not just a hopeful gamble, but a strategic move in a game we were becoming increasingly equipped to win.

Summoned to appear before the Board, we sensed an obvious tension in the room; it was clear that not all committee members were eager to endorse our plea. Undeterred, I laid out the trans-

formative journey Johnny had undertaken—his disciplined training, his impeccable conduct, and his undeniable progress over the
preceding months.

The Board members weighed my words with thoughtful deliber-
ation. And then, with a stern caveat that left no room for misin-
terpretation, they issued their verdict: Johnny would be reinstated,
but any future lapse in judgment or violation of rules would result
in irrevocable consequences.

Looking back, I sensed Mr. Smith might have had some doubts
about my ability to manage Johnny effectively. If so, his scepticism
wasn't entirely misplaced. There were numerous occasions later
on when Johnny's behaviour veered off course, making me wonder
if my life would have been easier—if not better—had the Board
declined to reinstate his license.

It's a thought that nagged at me during our rough patches, a haunt-
ing question that surfaced in the quiet moments when I questioned
the path we were on. Yet, each time this uncertainty crossed my
mind, it also served as a catalyst, reminding me of the high stakes
and the volatile but enthralling journey we had undertaken.

They often say that the line between genius and madness is a fine
one, a saying that resonates deeply with anyone who has ventured
to guide a temperamental fighter, gifted with an innate genius for
the sport. As I reflect on our early days, a time that now seems
bathed in a golden hue, I can't help but admit that there seemed to
be an essence of truth in this adage.

During that initial phase of our journey, I believe we were in the
honeymoon period of our partnership, where Johnny's raw talent

shone brightest, untarnished by the trials that lay ahead. It was a time of hope, promise, and unspoken potential. We were both blissfully unaware of the storms that awaited us, caught up in the exhilarating whirlwind of shaping a champion.

Everything was unfolding seamlessly, and Johnny was indeed exhibiting his utmost discipline and dedication. Now, with his license reclaimed, the task ahead of me was to interest some promoter into giving us some work in the bustling boxing circuit. Little has been known about Johnny's early career before our alliance; the numerous bouts he fought during his youthful days remain largely unrecorded.

However, it is well established that he reigned as the Schoolboy Champion in the years 1931, 1932, and 1933. Not just a promising boxer, Johnny was a versatile athlete during his school years. I possess an article written by Mr. Frank Rose from the *Daily Express*, who ardently asserts that Cusick had the potential to excel as a professional footballer, had he ventured down that path.

While on the subject, it's pertinent to note that Mr. Rose played a pivotal role in setting Johnny on the path that would eventually lead him to become the reigning king in the featherweight division. However, those glory days were still a distant dream during those initial phases of his career.

To kickstart Johnny's career, I brought him to meet Mr. Rose, hoping he could help us connect with a potential promoter. Mr. Rose was kind enough to visit during one of Johnny's training sessions and he liked what he saw. He wrote a positive article about Johnny and introduced us to a promoter willing to organize

Johnny's first match under my management. This was the first step in what we hoped would be a fruitful journey in the boxing world.

At that time, Mr. Bob Wolfenden was orchestrating events at the Junction Stadium, and he arranged for Johnny's inaugural match to be against Arly Hollingsworth, a formidable opponent from Sheffield, who had previously reigned as the ex-Boy Scout world champion. Hollingsworth had proven his prowess in the ring, holding his ground against some of the most acclaimed fighters nationwide. I mention this to emphasize that Johnny wasn't being handed an easy fight; he was up against a genuine contender in his first bout.

We immediately threw ourselves into training, and by 29 September 1935, Johnny was ready to face his first real test in the ring.

I'll admit, anxiety gnawed at me during the lead-up to the match. Despite witnessing Johnny's prowess in the gym, I hadn't yet seen him spar in a real ring, and I couldn't shake the worry that I might have been too ambitious in pairing him with a seasoned boxer like Hollingsworth for his first fight.

But Johnny exhibited no nerves. His casual demeanour, seemingly unfazed by his formidable opponent, served as a much-needed boost to my own confidence. I was about to witness the full extent of Johnny's capabilities when faced with a genuine challenge.

As the bell clanged, signalling the onset of the first round, Hollingsworth stormed out of his corner, a whirlwind of unrestrained aggression and relentless punches coming from every conceivable angle.

Johnny, however, was a study in grace under pressure, a dancer deftly avoiding the brunt of a raging storm. Every move he made was a ballet of agility and precision, his every step leaving Hollingsworth grappling with nothing but air and growing frustration.

By the end of the electrifying first round, Johnny had transformed the ring into his stage, where he was both the choreographer and the lead, rendering Hollingsworth's brutish advances clumsy, almost pitiable.

As the second round dawned, a visibly frustrated Hollingsworth shifted gears, resorting to tactics that skirted the fine line between fierce competition and flagrant foul play. In the heat of a fierce clinch, their heads clashed—a ruthless move that saw Johnny sustaining a cut to his eye.

Remarkably, this would be the solitary occasion throughout Johnny's illustrious career where his skin would be breached in battle. The round culminated with Johnny asserting his dominance. As he retreated to our corner, a quick inspection revealed that the damage was superficial. Johnny's spirit was unbroken, his resolve steelier than ever, ready to turn the tide in a battle that was quickly becoming legendary.

As we tackled the bleeding, Johnny flashed a wry smile, shaking his head in amused disbelief at the unexpected turn of events. 'Well, that's a new one on me.' He chuckled, a lightness in his voice that belied the fiery determination sparking in his eyes. This wasn't a setback, but a challenge. One he would not allow to happen again.

With the sound of the bell heralding the start of the third round, a transformed Johnny emerged from his corner. It was as if the cut had unleashed a more primal, ferocious version of him. The audience could almost feel the shift in the air, a crackling energy that had everyone on the edge of their seats.

Hollingsworth, probably used to dictating the rhythm of the fight, found himself suddenly dancing to a tune dictated by Johnny. Each assault he attempted met a graceful, yet punishing counter from Johnny, a symphony of well-placed jabs and hooks that left Hollingsworth scrambling, desperate to regain his footing in a match that was slipping through his fingers.

As the round progressed, Johnny's dominance became more pronounced. It was like watching a seasoned maestro play a brutal, yet strangely beautiful symphony, his fists creating a rhythm of power and finesse that left the spectators entranced.

By the time the round reached its crescendo, Hollingsworth was no longer the formidable opponent he had been when he stepped into the ring. He was a man overwhelmed, a testament to the raw, untamed power and potential housed within Johnny 'Nipper' Cusick.

The fight stretched to the fullest extent, with every round seemingly tilting the scales more in Johnny's favour. Hollingsworth, albeit a formidable and seasoned contender, seemed almost grateful to find himself upright at the final bell.

When the referee decisively granted the victory to Johnny, a resonant cheer erupted from the crowd. Johnny had not only won but captivated the audience, announcing himself not as a newcomer but as a fresh and electrifying force in the boxing world.

We were over our first hurdle, and to say I was thrilled with John-ny's sleek execution in the ring would be an understatement. But amidst the glory of the first victory, a critical realization dawned on me: Johnny had a tendency to take a while to shift into high gear, a slow burn at the start that held a potential storm cloud of peril. This wasn't merely an observation but a glaring vulnerability that needed ironing out.

In those beginning bouts, this sluggish onset had cost him, invit-ing a few vicious blows that had me grappling with anxiety at the corners of the ring. Yet, Johnny embodied adaptability in its truest form. He harboured an innate understanding that persisting in this manner was akin to handing a loaded gun to his adversaries, particularly as he found himself facing fiercer competition, indi-viduals who were carving their own arduous paths to glory.

As he scaled that monumental ascent that lay before him, the one that promised not only triumph but a legendary status, Johnny 'Nipper' Cusick was shaping up to be a force that redefined resil-ience and determination in the world of boxing.

3

COUP DE GRÂCE

Moving forward, I made sure to keep Johnny actively engaged, sometimes scheduling fights as frequently as once a week. But an even graver issue than that of being a slow starter emerged, one that seemed almost insurmountable: his profound hatred of training.

This disdain seemed to grow with time, becoming more pronounced as he aged. Tragically, this resistance would signal the untimely decline of his career, at a point when many fighters his age were at the peak of their form.

In the early days of our partnership, this flaw was not so noticeable. By keeping him boxing regularly, I managed to give him no chance of getting out of condition, even though he wasn't really tested by any significant rivals for a good stretch. He seemed to take nothing out of himself in those early bouts.

The trouble was, as I mentioned at the beginning, Johnny, in his heart, hated the game he had chosen as his career. Many times, he would lean in, a far-off look in his eyes, and confide in me: 'Truth is, I don the this glove and fight not out of a fiery passion but because I seem to have a knack for it, a talent that edges out over others. Moreover, it promises a pot of gold at the end, should one manage to brave the steep climb to the top.' A stance that echoed more with subdued embers than a blazing fire, not quite what one would expect from a lad eyeing the championship.

But that was Johnny, an enigmatic figure and a paradox unto himself, consistently defying the archetypal boxer's mindset throughout his tumultuous journey.

Following a few minor victories, Johnny faced a formidable opponent in Morecambe: Syd Rose from Preston. Though Johnny secured the win on points, he consistently held that Rose gave him one of his most challenging bouts.

Moving on to our first significant money match. Some of us might still remember the young fighter who bested Johnny in that unsanctioned bout back in early 1934, an encounter that left Johnny fainting on the ground after the fight. This emerging talent was managed by Mr. Martin, a man known for placing hefty bets on his fighters.

Confident from his prior victory over Johnny, Nipper Mack and his manager felt they could replicate that success. Emboldened, they proposed a match with a wager of fifty pounds on the side. Needless to say, both Johnny and I eagerly seized this chance to redeem ourselves and turn the tides in our favour.

At the time, a promoter, Mr. Harry Furness, was orchestrating matches at the Regent Sporting Club in Salford and recognized the potential of this bout as a major draw. Confident in its success, he secured the date for the third of November 1935. I fronted twenty pounds to cover our part of the bet, with the understanding that the balance would be handed over to the promoter before the fighters stepped into the ring. Yet, in a surprising twist, Mr. Martin hesitated at the eleventh hour, choosing not to place the remainder of the bet. Perhaps he sensed the upcoming tide of the match.

Thus, the stakes were set at the initial twenty pounds deposit, accompanied by a purse of ten pounds for the victor and five pounds for the runner-up.

In the realm of boxing, it's customary for the promoter to match the side bet with a purse, but I must admit, I was still navigating the ropes of these arrangements back then.

As for the anticipated face-off with Mack, what many anticipated as a nail-biter turned out to be a completely one-sided match. The only thing I can say about this bout is that while Nipper Mack showed heart and tenacity, he was no match for a dominant Johnny.

Throughout the full fifteen, two-minute rounds, Mack found himself consistently on the defensive. Either Johnny had vastly improved since their last encounter or Mack had notably declined.

Just weeks earlier, Mr. Jack Green showcased a premier event at the Brunswick Stadium in Leeds. The marquee matchups featured four of the nation's elite bantamweights. Len Hampston, recognized as the top contender for the bantam title, squared off against Bobby Magee. In another much-anticipated bout, George Marsden went toe-to-toe with Leeds's own Billy Miller. Each of these fighters had impressive records, making it a tightly contested showcase with no clear favourite.

I knew that Johnny would eventually have to face these fighters if we aspired to challenge for the bantam weight title. Convincing Johnny to join me in Leeds to watch them wasn't easy. He rarely showed interest in other bouts unless they were high-profile. Yet, I emphasized the significance of assessing these two matches, hinting at my plans to possibly line him up against one of them. Johnny, for all his indifference to watching others, had a sharp eye for gauging a boxer's skill, particularly when it came to someone in his weight and class.

After seeing both of these contests, I asked him what he thought his chances were against any of them. True to his nature, Johnny, ever humble and never one to exaggerate, responded, 'I believe I can take on Marsden, Miller, and Hampston, but don't bother with Magee. He's too clever and could make anyone look a fool.'

Moving forward with those matches, Johnny and I found ourselves deep in strategizing. We mulled over our options, deciding the best approach to entice one of these contenders into the ring.

Setting our sights on Marsden, given his recent surge in popularity around Manchester and his commendable showings, we thought it apt to approach his manager for a bout.

Marsden had been making quite the impression on the local boxing aficionados, especially after he clinched a victory over the reigning Belle Vue champion, Johnny King. Fully aware of the leap in competition Johnny would be facing, I anticipated some eyebrows raised at our audacity to challenge a boxer of Marsden's stature.

I concocted a plan to publicly challenge Marsden through the press, even going so far as to put money on Johnny's victory, albeit a modest sum.

The boxing community treated our audacious callout as little more than a joke. Whispers and chuckles about 'sending Johnny to his doom' echoed in response.

Marsden and his manager, seemingly buoyed by a cocktail of amusement and confidence, seemed to view this as a ripe opportunity. They accepted the challenge, with one caveat: my conviction had to be backed by a fifty-pound wager on the match's outcome.

After discussing the proposition with Johnny, we agreed that if staking fifty pounds was what it took to seal the deal, then so be it. Merely three weeks after his bout with Nipper Mack, Johnny was set to face Marsden at the Junction Stadium. On the evening of the seventeenth of November 1935, they squared off in a ring surrounded by a sea of spectators.

Almost unanimously, the crowd seemed convinced I'd lost my mind, throwing Johnny in the ring with such a formidable foe. The odds-makers wasted no time in making their predictions clear, stacking the deck heavily against Johnny with odds of four to one. Remarkably, there weren't many takers. I did capitalize on these favourable odds a bit, ensuring our even-money wager appeared all the more enticing in the betting circles.

The bell signalled the start of the first round, and what ensued was nothing short of intense drama.

Marsden stepped into the ring, all guns blazing, clearly set on swiftly ending the bout and humbling the up-and-coming contender.

From the get-go, he had Johnny on the ropes, landing punch after punch throughout the entirety of the round. I'll admit, my heart was in my throat until the bell finally marked the round's end. Once again, Johnny's habitual slow start had made him vulnerable, giving Marsden ample opportunity to dominate.

To the uninitiated spectator, it surely seemed the bout wouldn't last beyond three rounds. Indeed, during the interval, murmurs around the ringside grew louder, with many betting that the fight wouldn't see its final round.

As Johnny returned to the corner, sweat dripping from his brow and the redness from the initial onslaught evident on his face, I implored him, 'Johnny, use the ring more. Let him tire out. Dance around him until he runs out of steam.'

Seeing the worried expression on my face, Johnny smiled at me and said, 'Don't worry. I'm all right. I'll knock the steam out of him and save time.'

True to his word, as the second round commenced. Marsden charged Johnny with a gleam of overconfidence, unleashing a ferocious right swing aimed to end the bout. But Johnny, with agility and precision, dodged the swing and, in one fluid motion, landed a flawless left hook. The impact was so great that Marsden went down, hitting the canvas as if he'd been poleaxed.

The arena went silent for a split second before erupting into whispers and gasps. From my vantage point, I could see the pure astonishment painted on Marsden's face. He might have been mentally preparing for victory, but definitely not for this. He struggled to his feet after the referee's count, his eyes no longer filled with the same confidence.

Though he managed to endure the round, the momentum had decidedly shifted. Johnny dominated the arena, and Marsden, despite his commendable resilience, was on the receiving end for the remainder of the bout.

As the rounds progressed, Johnny's prowess became undeniably evident. Johnny's victory was indisputable, and the referee didn't hesitate a moment before declaring the outcome.

As the final bell rang, the same spectators who had earlier doubted Johnny's decision to face Marsden were now on their feet, applauding his exceptional display. It was evident to promoters that he had captured the fans' hearts.

This shift in sentiment catapulted us from seekers to the sought-after.

After engaging in two relatively minor bouts within the next couple of weeks, Johnny was paired against the second boxer we had previously scouted in Leeds.

On the sixteenth of December, Belle Vue had organized a charity event, and they approached me to have Johnny face off against Billy Miller from Leeds. This marked Johnny's debut with Manchester's top-tier promotions. It's worth noting that Johnny Cusick wasn't a creation of Belle Vue's grooming—he didn't have the luxury of hometown advantages. He carved his legacy through relentless away matches, proving his mettle time and again.

In addition, and within few days, I inked a deal for him to box Len Hampston in Leeds on 30 January 1936.

The match between Cusick and Miller spanned ten rounds, with Johnny effortlessly securing a win on points. The only voice of discontent post-match was Tom Hurst, Miller's manager. He promptly sought a rematch upon hearing the referee's decision, even proposing to extend it to a twelve-round face-off.

At the time, Johnny was a mere seventeen, and boxing regulations stipulated that fighters under eighteen could only participate in matches limited to ten three-minute rounds.

Interestingly, Johnny's eighteenth birthday was on 27 January— only three days before his contest with Hampson. But Tom Hurst, hungry for a rematch before the Hampson fight, posed a slight conundrum. To accommodate Hurst's wishes for an extended match, we creatively adjusted Johnny's birthday to 17 January, allowing the fight to span more than the customary ten rounds.

Hurst believed the elongated duration would work in Miller's favour, assuming Johnny would tire. The bout took place in Black-pool on the seventeenth of January, and he was to find out that the shoe was on the other foot. It was Miller who flagged. Hurst's strategy only afforded Miller a more thorough defeat. That succinctly sums up the essence of the rematch.

Now, in less than 2 weeks, Johnny will be facing Len Hampston— the third contender from the initial quartet we had observed. This bout was seen as the defining moment. Yet, the familiar chorus of sceptics chimed in, suggesting I was recklessly placing my fighter in harm's way.

Hampston's supporters were eagerly pursuing me with bets, and in haste, I prematurely accepted odds of six to four on Cusick's victory. Had I been patient until the fight day, our winnings could have been doubled, as staggering three-to-one odds against Johnny were being offered right at the ringside. However, among bettors there's an adage: 'The worst of the odds, the best of the settling,' and this was getting to be a habit with Johnny and me.

The day of the fight arrived, bringing with it an unexpected hiccup during the weigh-in. Johnny tipped the scales one pound over the stipulated weight. Baffled, I could only assume that perhaps my trainer had miscalculated somewhere. Distressed by this oversight, we immediately whisked Johnny to the baths. Following a steaming bath and an intensive rub-down, we made a swift return. This time, Johnny met the weight requirement right on the mark.

As rumours of Johnny's initial weight misstep began to permeate the betting circles, the mood shifted noticeably. Excited whispers and speculative glances followed as bettors, sensing an opportunity, started placing their stakes heavily on Hampston.

Amidst this growing uncertainty, Johnny approached me with a determined look in his eyes. 'Seems like the odds are shifting, huh?' he remarked casually, a wry smile hinting at his unfazed demeanour.

I nodded, watching the flurry of activity around us. 'Yeah, Hampston's now the hot favourite.'

Unperturbed by the shift in the betting landscape, Johnny maintained his characteristic confidence. He leaned closer, his voice firm and resolute. 'Put my share of the prize money on me,' he said with unwavering belief in his victory.

As the bell rang, a familiar dread washed over me, reminding me of the tumultuous beginning of the Marsden contest. Johnny's recurring Achilles' heel, an almost deliberate vulnerability, showed up again, almost as if he were inadvertently daring Hampston to take a swing. And Hampston, seizing the moment, dominated the ring, launching Cusick into a defensive spiral.

He succeeded in flouring Johnny twice, albeit briefly. It was a harrowing sight for any manager, seeing their fighter in such a position.

When Johnny later confided in me at the corner that he was more startled than harmed, it did offer some solace. Yet, the weight of concern was undeniable, and every second of that round felt like an eternity. The bell that marked its conclusion was a sweet reprieve, and I found myself silently thanking it for its timely intervention.

The atmosphere was electric, a cacophony of excitement and expectation. Echoing in the backdrop, I could discern voices confidently predicting that the fight wouldn't last beyond three rounds. My nerves were frayed, and I suspect my anxiety was palpable. Yet, amidst this chaos, Johnny remained the eye of the storm. With reassuring calm, he looked me in the eye, stating with unwavering certainty, 'He won't catch me again.'

As the bell rang to signal the start of the second round, a resolute Hampston surged forward, clearly eager to bring the fight to a swift conclusion. However, the Cusick that faced him now was a transformed fighter.

Despite Hampston's fervent attempts, he couldn't land the decisive blow everyone anticipated. Instead, Johnny artfully manoeuvred around the ring, deftly deploying his left hand to deflect Hampston's aggressive, yet increasingly futile, punches. By the time the bell signalled the end of the round, Johnny was not just defending himself; he was asserting his dominance.

Sitting in his corner, with a confident smirk, he whispered, 'I've got his measure. Don't worry.'

As the third round commenced, Johnny's prowess truly began to shine. He dazzled the audience with exquisite boxing techniques and nimble footwork. The round's performance unequivocally communicated that this wasn't going to be the one-sided match it initially seemed.

When it came to pure boxing finesse, Johnny was in a league of his own, overshadowing Hampston completely. By the round's close, it was evident to all that Johnny had clinched it decisively. He confided in me during the break, a sheen of sweat on his brow but his eyes alight with the thrill of the fight. Leaning in, he shared with me, his voice a low rumble over the din of the crowd.

'He's burning out fast,' Johnny said, nodding towards a visibly fatigued Hampston. 'His energy's dropping quicker than he expected. We've got this.'

Notably absent were the earlier voices confidently betting on Hampston— the once-vocal crowd of gamblers had fallen eerily silent.

During the fourth round, Johnny's prowess was on full display, building upon the momentum he had gathered in the preceding round. Hampston, visibly struggling, was attempting to pin down a target that seemed perpetually out of reach. His mounting frustration was evident, leading him to adopt a more aggressive yet imprecise approach, hoping to regain a footing in the bout. However, this played right into Johnny's strengths.

As the bell signalled the end of the round, an undeniable realization settled over the audience: unless something drastically changed, the outcome of this match was becoming evident.

Those once-bold judges, who had freely laid out heavy odds against Johnny, were now in a frenzied rush to back him. The tables had turned, and the whispers of their prior convictions were drowned by their hasty attempts to salvage a bad wager. As for placing bets on Hampston? Enthusiasm seemed to have dwindled, with scant takers willing to bank on his win. Those who had gambled against Johnny were now in a tight spot. As the fighters squared up for the fifth round, which would be the climax of the bout, those bettors had little hope of salvaging their ill-placed wagers.

Hampston, it seemed, had been fed a narrative that Johnny's right hand was his Achilles heel—a mere distraction and not a weapon of any real consequence. Maybe Johnny himself had craftily perpetuated this myth, judiciously holding back his right, allowing his adversary to underestimate its potency.

This oversight was to be the very snare that would entangle Hampston.

As the rounds progressed, you could sense a growing confidence in Hampston's approach. Perhaps believing he had unlocked the secret to defeating Johnny, he became more aggressive. The arena was thick with anticipation as spectators leaned forward in their seats, sensing a pivotal moment was about to unfold.

But Johnny, ever the ring tactician, was setting the stage. Seemingly retreating, luring Hampston into a false sense of security, he was in reality positioning his unsuspecting prey. Each step back was a calculated move, each dodge an invitation, waiting, just waiting, for Hampston to spot that 'golden opportunity' to unleash the fight-ending blow.

As the tension in the arena reached its zenith, it played out just as Johnny had anticipated.

Midway through the round, Hampston, spotting what he believed to be a golden opportunity, lunged forward, confident of his impending victory. But in that split-second, the narrative took a drastic turn.

Johnny unleashed a right cross, a punch so perfectly timed and executed that the following day's headlines would dub it the 'dream punch.'

The impact was immediate and devastating. Hampston crashed to the canvas, reminiscent of a mighty tree felled in its prime.

The audience held its collective breath as the referee began the ritualistic count.

With sheer willpower, Hampston managed to haul himself up by the count of nine, embodying the spirit of a true fighter. But the aftermath of that 'dream punch' was too much to bear. Legs wobbly and senses disoriented, he fell down once more, without being touched.

Mr. Jack Hart, the referee, made a decision that puzzled many onlookers. Instead of declaring Johnny the immediate winner by knockout, he chose to start the count again, offering Hampston what seemed like an unexpected second chance.

'One...two...three...' Hart's voice echoed through the arena, each count deliberate and clear.

The crowd watched in suspense as Hampston lay on the canvas, struggling to regain his bearings.

'Four...five...six...'

Hampston began to stir, his efforts to rise visible but laboured.

'Seven...'

With a display of sheer willpower that bordered on the miraculous, Hampston pushed himself up.

'Eight!' Hart announced, just as Hampston staggered to his feet, wobbling and dazed.

But it was evident to everyone watching that he was a shadow of his former self. Hampston, now upright, was clearly a spent force, like a ship adrift without sails.

Johnny, sensing his moment and with the precision of a seasoned hunter, landed a swift left hook. It was the coup de grâce.

Hampston went down, this time with no hope of rising.

The subsequent count was but a formality, culminating in a total count of twenty-seven over the fallen fighter. But in that electric moment, the specifics of the count seemed trivial. Victory was Johnny's, and the euphoria was all that mattered.

The arena erupted into chaotic jubilation. Cheers, shouts, and applause filled the air, as if a dam of restrained emotion had burst forth. Spectators jumped to their feet, their faces a mix of elation and disbelief.

That evening, Johnny didn't just win a bout; he etched an indelible mark in the annals of boxing history.

As the echoes of the evening's excitement subsided, a singular notion cemented itself in my consciousness: Johnny had to be the next contender for the championship title. With such a commanding victory over Hampston, the previous frontrunner for the Title shot, it seemed only logical to me that Johnny would ascend to take that coveted spot.

We assumed the path ahead was clear and straightforward.

The Board, however, had different plans in store. They orchestrated a series of elimination bouts involving the top contenders from various regions.

To our surprise, Johnny was slated to face George Marsden once more. This was perplexing, considering Johnny had decisively defeated Marsden less than three months ago, leaving no room for doubt in anyone's mind about the outcome.

Further compounding the situation, Hampston was handed a direct entry to the final. This meant that, should Johnny successfully advance, he would be faced with the daunting task of squaring off against and defeating Hampston yet again before he could challenge for the champion title—a scenario both frustrating and challenging for Johnny.

Upon the announcement of this decision, we were plunged into tumultuous times. Cusick, with a sense of righteous indignation, felt targeted by the Board, and I wholeheartedly shared his sentiment. For a while, his frustrations rendered him almost unreachable to me. This marked the onset of our numerous challenges, and it was this incident that triggered Cusick's rebellious streak.

When the ink dried on the contracts for Johnny to face Ellis Ashurst at the Junction Stadium in Manchester, spirits were high. Mere two weeks after his bout with Hampston, Johnny claimed a KO victory over Ashurst in the seventh rounds.

The impending match against Marsden loomed on the twenty-fourth of February 1936, offering us a comfortable two-week preparation window.

4

THE VANISHING ACT

J ohnny's commitment waxed and waned; at times, he was intensely dedicated, sweating through rigorous sessions, and at others, he seemed distant and uninterested, vocally expressing his reluctance.

All appeared to be falling into place—his weight was on target; his training was progressing—until the day prior to the fight. That's when chaos descended.

Believing it prudent, I had arranged for Johnny to lodge with his trainer to pre-empt any unexpected missteps. But I was met with a jarring phone call that morning: Johnny had vanished. Stealthily, he'd awoken at the crack of dawn while the household was still engulfed in slumber and made his silent exit. The trainer had been scouring the city for him since sunrise. Hours had passed, and yet there was no sign of Johnny.

What a predicament I found myself in! After scouring the town, visiting all of Johnny's usual haunts, I felt a growing despair. His absence wasn't just an inconvenience; it jeopardized his budding career and our collective efforts.

In a last-ditch attempt, I sought help from his mother, highlighting the gravity of the situation and how much was riding on Johnny's upcoming match.

That morning, Johnny awoke with a restless spirit, driven by an inscrutable yearning to detach. While everyone was still asleep, he decided to head out. He started with a walk through the familiar streets of his childhood. These winding lanes held many a memory of simpler times, when dreams of becoming a champion were just that—dreams, distant and unreachable.

Stopping by a side road cafe, he enjoyed this wet, grey and cold wintery day with a hot cup of tea and hearty double English breakfast—fried eggs, bacon, sausage, baked beans, grilled toma- toes, and plenty of buttered toasts. This wasn't the diet of a boxer on the eve of a crucial match, but Johnny enjoyed every bite, this taste of the world outside the ring.

Next, he found himself heading out of town. He had always been drawn to the quiet serenity of nature. Walking through the fields under the drizzly rain and hearing nothing but the wind brought a peace that the clamour of the gym could never offer.

It was a connection to a time before the world knew his name, before every move, every word, and every decision were scrutinised.

In a village pub, he had a hearty lunch, indulging in a large portion of fish and chips, taking his time to savour the moment. That was followed by a sticky toffee pudding and a few pints to wash it down.

A few locals recognised him and approached cautiously. Instead of discussing boxing, they chatted about the weather, local news, and shared laughs over trivial matters.

As the day turned to evening, Johnny found a quiet spot overlooking the ship canal. He sat there, reflecting on his journey so far. All the sweat, the blood, the tears. The highs of victory and the lows of defeat. He allowed himself to be vulnerable, letting out tears that had been pent up for too long.

The weight of reality began to push down on Johnny. Instead of returning to the hectic environment awaiting him, Johnny sought solace in one of the few places he felt he could truly be himself: an old friend's home. Derek, a childhood mate, had been with him through thick and thin. Their bond had been forged long before boxing entered Johnny's life, in days filled with scraped knees, makeshift football games, and shared secrets.

Derek lived in an older part of town, in a cosy home with creaky wooden floors and the comforting smell of aged wood. The moment Johnny knocked on the door, and Derek saw the vulnerability in his eyes, he knew Johnny needed a haven, no questions asked. He ushered Johnny inside, making him a cuppa and settling him down in the familiar living room, where many of their past confessions had been exchanged.

Johnny didn't speak much. He just savoured the familiarity, the escape. Derek, sensing this need, simply sat with him, the comforting presence of an old friend more therapeutic than any words could have been. The hours slipped by, with both of them occasionally reminiscing about old memories or simply basking in the comfortable silence.

It was only when Derek's phone rang, with a frantic call from Johnny's mother, that they realized the gravity of Johnny's disappearance, and the panic in their voices was palpable.

The fight, the preparations, the reputation—everything was at stake.

Understanding the urgency, Derek gently reminded Johnny of the responsibilities he had, not just to himself but to everyone who believed in him, everyone who had invested their time, money, and faith in his talent. Derek's words, combined with the grounding effect of their time spent together, seemed to work on Johnny.

When I arrived at Derek's doorstep, Johnny, while still weighed down by his personal battles, was at least ready to face the external ones.

But, when we returned to the gym, a new obstacle presented itself. I was flabbergasted when the scales revealed he was a whopping seven pounds overweight with just a day left to the fight. It felt like the universe was playing a cruel joke on us; the challenge ahead seemed almost insurmountable.

He expressed his regrets and assured me he'd shed the weight immediately. While I harboured reservations about his ability to do so, I believed it was worth an attempt. After all, presenting him at the weigh-in with that excess weight would undoubtedly land both of us in hot water with the Board of Control

Time and again, I've been astounded by his resilience—how he could endure ten or twelve rounds in the ring, especially given the manner in which he would push himself to the brink.

All told, Johnny went through twenty rigorous rounds of boxing and training that evening, mere hours before he was set to face a well-conditioned opponent for another fifteen rounds.

We managed to get him down to the mandated weight of eight stones six pounds, but how he remained standing, and even more so, boxed effectively to secure the verdict, remains an enduring mystery to me.

We reached Nottingham just in time for the weigh-in. Once Johnny had passed the weight requirement, I rushed him to our hotel. Following a light lunch, I had him rest, holding onto the hope that a few hours of sleep might replenish the energy he'd lost during his intense weight-cutting session.

I endured a distressing afternoon and evening, anxiously awaiting the start of the fight. To me, Johnny appeared in poor shape, and I couldn't shake the feeling that everyone, including his opponent, could plainly see he was far from being in optimal condition for the contest.

Finally, the bout began, and I won't delve into a detailed blow-by-blow account of each round. I don't think that I have ever watched such a dull contest in my life.

If Marsden had begun as he did in their initial contest, I'm certain he could have stopped Johnny. To this day, I'm amazed he didn't recognize he had a dead man in front of him.

I surmise that Marsden hadn't shaken off the memory of the thrashing he received from Johnny during their initial encounter about three months ago, deciding to take no chances. Thus, the ring bore witness to a curious spectacle: there we had two boys in the ring, one unable to do anything, and the other unwilling to try and do something.

For all fifteen rounds, Johnny continually feigned offense, suggesting an imminent attack, yet never truly mustering the strength to follow through. As the fight finally concluded, Johnny was declared the victor, and no one seemed to dispute the decision. Marsden could only blame himself for the loss. Opportunity had practically been handed to him, yet he missed his moment to seize it.

The simple truth is that on that occasion, Johnny had got away with murder.

5

ALMOST UNBEATABLE!

At that time, Johnny was a sought-after name in the sport. Less than two weeks later, on 5 March 1936, he found himself back in the Liverpool ring, squaring off against Mog Mason, the bantamweight champion of Wales. However, Mason was no match for Johnny's prowess. Outclassing him at every turn, Johnny secured a resounding victory, winning comfortably on points.

I was wholly convinced that, at this stage in his career, Johnny was almost unbeatable. I would have confidently matched him against any contender globally within his weight class. He had this uncanny ability to make boxing appear so easy and effortless. And listening afterwards to so many of his victims, he was almost unhittable in the ring.

On the twenty-third of March, Johnny returned to the Leeds Town Hall for another bout. He was up against Fred Morris, the bantamweight champion of Southern Eire. Morris was an exceptional boxer, every bit a formidable opponent. That evening, the spectators and I were treated to one of the most skilful matches I've ever seen.

Johnny was at his absolute best, but Morris never let him get too comfortable or create much distance in their battle. Both fighters received thunderous applause from the audience. It was truly a shame there had to be a loser.

Based on his remarkable performance, many drew comparisons between Johnny and the legendary Jim Driscoll.

For Johnny and I, it marked yet another step closer to the bantamweight title.

Now, I turn to the final contender among the four we had observed just half a year prior: Bobby Magee.

The esteemed Mr. Harry Farrand was organizing a charity event to benefit the Manchester Royal Infirmary. He approached me, hoping to have Johnny featured on the bill against a chosen opponent. Ever eager to support a worthy cause, Johnny was quick to agree. So, without any knowledge of our upcoming adversary, I committed by signing the contract.

Clearly, Mr. Farrand had picked up on the whispers about Johnny's reservations concerning Bobby Magee. This probably motivated him to have me ink the contracts without disclosing the identity of our forthcoming opponent.

I have to concede, they pulled a fast one over me with that move. But when I learned who Johnny would be facing, my concern was minimal. The lad would have to be extraordinarily talented to halt Johnny's winning streak.

Eight days after facing Morris, on the thirty-first of March, Johnny stepped into the ring at Junction Stadium in Manchester.

He vindicated my belief in him with a resounding knockout in the seventh round.

Bobby Magee was likely the most skilled boxer Johnny had encountered up to that point. If Magee had pursued boxing with a deeper commitment, he certainly had the potential for greatness—he possessed all the qualities of a champion.

Johnny took a liking to this boy, and for a while, I had him as a sparring partner for Johnny in one or two pivotal contests. However, I soon realized that Bobby was bad news for Johnny. When I wasn't watching and Magee was around, serious training took a backseat. I genuinely liked the boy myself, but having two fighters with the same temperament in the same stable is asking for trouble. For Johnny's own sake, I had to separate them.

Our subsequent match pitted us against Ken Barret from Wales. Johnny triumphed with a knockout in the seventh round. This set the stage for what would become one of the defining fights in Johnny's career.

He was paired against Jackie Brown at Belle Vue on 18 May 1936. The victor of this bout would face Len Hampston in the final eliminator, determining the challenger for the bantam championship against Johnny King.

Brown, now twenty-six years old, trained at Belle Vue gymnasium, and trained hard. He was a controversial figure with fiery temperament. Less than two years ago, in July 1934, he faced a four-month sentence with hard labour for biting a man's ear off in a Blackpool hotel during a heated argument over a girl.

Johnny's training intensity was unparalleled. To him, Brown was the pinnacle in boxing during that era. And, I should mention, Johnny had reservations about his odds against Jackie. Interestingly, I felt confident in Johnny's ability to triumph over Brown. Still, it was refreshing to witness Johnny's dedication in his training for this match.

A supremely conditioned Johnny stepped onto the scales on the day of the weigh-in. With both fighters making weight, everything was poised for a magnificent showdown. In hindsight, I'm confident that the audience left without a shred of disappointment that evening.

Johnny's recent performances and his impressive winning streak had garnered him a solid base of fans, many of whom shared my optimism about his prospects against Brown. With the venue filled to capacity, both fighters stepped into the ring to the resounding cheers from their combined supporters.

As they faced one another in the ring, waiting for the referee's instructions Brown smiled at Cusick.

'How old are you, son?' he asked.

'Eighteen' replied Cusick.

'Never mind,' said Brown. 'I'll look after you.'

But Cusick needed no looking after. He was well equipped to take care of him-self.

Before the match, betting was intense, with Brown being the slight favourite at odds of five to four.

What a spirited contest it turned out to be! In the initial rounds, Johnny seemed to have the upper hand, but as the fight reached its midpoint, Brown had showcased impressive skills, making it a challenge to forecast the victor. The match continued with the advantage shifting between the two, ensuring there wasn't a single dull moment.

This was my assessment of the bout leading up to the twelfth round when Johnny truly shined. He landed some heavy hits on Brown, and I firmly believe that if not for the bell's intervention, Jackie might have been floored. The thirteenth round had Brown emerging from his corner, as feisty as before, with neither boxer yielding an inch. I've witnessed less actions in entire ten-round matches than what these two delivered in this single round.

As the fourteenth round commenced, Johnny continued his dominance. Near its conclusion, he landed a series of solid right-hand punches on Brown, who found himself pinned against the ropes, taking blow after blow. Once again, the bell seemed to come to Brown's rescue, potentially saving him from a knockout.

As they met centre ring to touch gloves before the final round, the crowd was in a frenzy of anticipation. Brown's resilience showcased his calibre as a fighter. I genuinely believed Johnny would finish him off in this concluding round.

As with all great moments, the fight eventually came to its conclusion, and without hesitation, the referee declared Johnny the victor.

A commotion erupted in Brown's corner.

His manager, ever the showman, leaped into the ring, challenging the referee's decision. Almost instantly, multiple altercations broke out near Brown's corner.

I'm convinced that the manager's impulsive reaction was the catalyst for the chaos that ensued. It took a full twenty minutes, and the intervention of a police escort, before both fighters could safely exit the ring. Without a shadow of doubt in my mind, Johnny deserved that victory. He had clearly done enough to earn the win.

Mr. Lumiansky, Brown's manager, didn't stop there. He escalated the matter to the Board. Subsequently, we were summoned for a hearing. After thorough scrutiny of his complaint, the Board upheld the referee's decision. Yet, both Johnny and I couldn't shake off a feeling of dissatisfaction with how everything transpired.

After discussing the situation, Johnny proposed offering Brown a rematch. He leaned in, saying, 'I got the verdict, but how I'll never know.' His voice was tinged with an unusual blend of humility and perplexity. He shook his head, the motion slow. 'All the commotion, all the fuss...' he trailed off, then lifted his gaze, his decision clear in his resolute expression. 'Forget it. I'd fight him again.' He continued with a firm voice, 'I'm confident I can secure a more definitive victory next time, leaving no room for doubt.'

In concurrence with his perspective, we approached the Board to suggest a follow-up match with Brown, hoping it would clear our path to contend for the title.

The Board commended Johnny for his sportsmanship, while also highlighting to both of us that we were under no obligation to offer Brown a rematch.

Mr. Smith, from the Board, later confided in me, asserting that my decision was ill-advised. He implied that if the roles were reversed, the other party might not have extended the same courtesy. As events unfolded, it became evident just how astute Mr. Smith's insights were regarding the boxing world and its intricacies. His words about the unpredictable nature of fighters and managers would resonate deeply with me, as I was to be vividly reminded in the ensuing weeks.

In just a matter of days, on 27 May 1936, we struck an agreement with promoter Bob Wolfenden, and it was decided that the bout would unfold at the Junction Stadium on the thirteenth of July.

As soon as we made our intentions to face Brown again public through the media, promoters were eagerly vying for the chance to host this much-anticipated fight.

Brown wasted no time and began his training that very day. He then relocated to special training quarters in the Lake District. Cusick spent the weekend at the coast in Llandudno before he kicked off his own training schedule.

With a good two months to ensure optimal fitness for this fight, I secured training accommodations for Johnny along with a team of half a dozen sparring partners at Hollingworth Lake.

Remarkably, Johnny was back at the venue where he'd had his inaugural match under my management just shy of ten months prior. But the contrasts were stark! For this bout, Johnny's purse amounted to five hundred pounds, with an additional twenty two percent of the gate. This was a significant leap from the mere five pounds the same promoter had compensated Johnny for that initial fight not even a year earlier.

Regrettably, not everything went as hoped.

Johnny swiftly adapted to his new training environment, accompanied by his coach and sparring partners. Initially, I made it a point to visit the 'camp' every alternate day. However, as training progressed and became more intense, I ensured I was with him every evening as soon as my business affairs permitted. For a considerable duration, everything appeared to be progressing smoothly and according to our laid-out plan.

On the eve of the fight, I spent the entire evening with Johnny. As he retired for the night, I departed, leaving everyone in high spirits. I assured Johnny I'd return early the following day to accompany him for the weigh-in.

I reached Johnny's place around 10 a.m. and immediately had him step on the scales to ensure his weight was on track. Everything looked promising. By 11 a.m., he was merely three ounces over the limit, which seemed ideal. Given the three hours remaining until the official weigh-in at 2 p.m., we expected Johnny to be roughly half a pound under the eight stones and six pounds limit by that time.

Regarding the events that followed, I genuinely believe Johnny was completely blameless. From the moment I had him step on the scales until he did so again at 2 p.m., he never left my sight. Yet we were in for a staggering revelation. The Board Official informed me that Johnny exceeded the limit by a pound. Despite re-weighing him, I remained sceptical about the scale's accuracy. It's one of those inexplicable occurrences, and even after so many years, I'm still not entirely persuaded that he truly surpassed the bantam weight limit.

The venue erupted in chaos, and it wasn't long before the validity of Mr. Smith's caution became abundantly clear, reinforcing his earlier sentiment about my naivety.

Mr. Lumiansky, Brown's manager, wasted no time in making his stance clear. He insisted on new contracts and demanded an immediate hundred-pound forfeit from my side. Only after meeting these conditions would he even entertain the idea of discussing a bout with an overweight contender.

In my state of confusion and disbelief, I spent the entire hour allotted for Johnny to shed the extra pound just arguing. On top of this, we were also bound by a significant weight forfeit to the promoter. With this predicament looming over us, we were entirely at their mercy.

What Mr. Lumiansky failed to recognize was that Johnny had graciously given his fighter another opportunity. And now, because of the weigh-in debacle, we had unwittingly relinquished our right to proceed towards that coveted title bout.

Mr. Lumiansky had the power to let the fight proceed under the original terms of the purse. Considering the fight was already a sell-out, there was no legitimate reason to reduce Johnny's portion of the earnings. Yet, given his nature, Brown's manager meant to have his pound of flesh.

The promoter insisted that I lower the offer to seventeen and a half percent of the gate, to which I reluctantly agreed. While Brown's manager technically acted within his rights, his actions seemed a rather ungracious response to Johnny's generosity in granting Brown a rematch.

Under the revised terms, Johnny's share amounted to three hundred and eleven pounds, but after accounting for the hundred pounds forfeit and covering hotel and training expenses, by the time everyone was settled, both Johnny and I found ourselves at a financial loss. Not only did we miss the chance for the bantam title match, but we were also unjustly deprived of a favourable verdict.

Even with the unexpected twist of Johnny being declared over-weight, the anticipation for the fight hadn't diminished.

As the night unfolded, both fighters made their entrance to a roaring, packed house. The underlying tension between the two camps had electrified the atmosphere, making the crowd all the more eager to witness the bout's outcome. The betting frenzy was at its peak, with both fighters pegged at even odds, resulting in sizable wagers and a flurry of money changing hands.

The bell heralded the start, and immediately Brown sprung into action, exhibiting his usual flair. However, a discerning eye might have noticed an added measure of caution, perhaps a newfound respect for Johnny's capabilities.

Both fighters showcased exemplary technique, and the initial rounds seemed to oscillate evenly between the two, with neither establishing a dominant lead. As the rounds progressed, it became evident that Johnny had drawn lessons from their last encounter. He deftly utilized a pristine left jab, breaking through Brown's once-impenetrable guard. As the match unfolded, Brown increasingly struggled to sidestep the precision and power of that punishing left.

The fight continued, with Johnny masterfully anticipated and countered each of Brown's manoeuvres, steadily amassing a formidable lead in points. From my vantage point, it seemed that Johnny dominated each round from the fourth through the twelfth. The sentiment was apparently shared by the betting crowd; by this juncture, odds of five to one were being laid against Brown.

A close friend of mine, who despite our friendship, had initially backed Brown with a sizable bet at even odds, served as testament to the changing winds of the match. Yet, by the fourteenth round, this very individual was laying odds five to one in favour of Johnny. It's rare for a professional bettor to shift so dramatically without substantial justification.

As the dust settled and the echoes of the final bell faded, tension filled the air. The crowd waited with bated breath, their expectations clear.

Then, to the sheer disbelief of the vast majority present, Brown was declared the winner.

The arena erupted in a mix of astonishment and dissent.

Subsequent to the bout, I was informed that the referee had given Brown the edge by a mere quarter of a point. Of all the verdicts I've witnessed throughout my years in the boxing realm, that one stands out as one of the most confounding.

Adding insult to injury, this came on the heels of an already tumultuous series of events.

JOHN CUSICK
FEATHERWEIGHT CHAMPION GREAT BRITAIN & BRITISH EMPIRE
MANAGER: JOHN BENNETT
"BRAEMAR": BIRCHINGTON ROAD, MANCHESTER 14
PHONES: DIDSBURY 2649 · PENDLETON 1055

JOHN CUSICK
NORTHERN AREA FEATHERWEIGHT CHAMPION
Manager: JOHN BENNETT
"Braemar" Birchington Road, Manchester, 14
Phones: Didsbury 2649; Pendleton 1055

Johnny 'Nipper' Cusick (27 January 1918 – 1 March 1990). Winner of the Northern England Area featherweight title in 1937, British featherweight title in 1938, and British Empire featherweight title in 1939.

John Bennett (middle) who was Johnny Cusick's manager from 1935 to 1947.

Cusick in the controversial fight with Jackie Brown on 18 May 1936 at Belle Vue, Manchester

Photo taken at the Grand Hotel, Manchester on 27 May 1936, when the contract for the Cusick – Brown rematch was signed. From left: Jackie Brown, Mr. Dave Lumiansky (Brown's manager), Mr. John Bennett (Cusick's manager), and Mr. R. Wolfenden, the promoter.

Johnny 'Nipper' Cusick defeated Eugene Peyre, France's featherweight champion, with a knockout in the tenth round on 6 March 1939 at King's Hall, Belle
Vue, Manchester. Manager John Bennet at the ringside (on the left).

The Duke and Duchess of Windsor were at the ringside when Johnny Cusick defeated Bernard Leroux, France's bantamweight champion, in Monte Carlo on 5 August
1939. In the centre, in light trousers, the Marquis of Queensberry, President of the
National Sporting Club, to his left are the Duchess and the Duke of Windsor.

Johnny Cusick with manager John Bennett on the train departing
to Monte Carlo on 3 August 1939

Johnny Cusick at work in 1970.
Picture taken from the Manchester Evening News, Weekend Magazine,
21 March 1970

6

AN INDOMITABLE SPIRIT

Our aspirations in the bantam division shattered, Johnny and I sat down for a heart-to-heart. After much contemplation, we agreed to shift our sights to the featherweight division. It felt like turning the clock back to square one, but with Johnny's undeniable skill, it didn't take long for us to stake our claim and earn our place in the more robust class.

In his debut bout as a featherweight, Johnny squared off against Bobby Hinds in Rotherham. Just five weeks post the tumultuous Brown saga, on the sixteenth of August, Johnny confidently secured a decisive victory, clinching a clear win on points.

On the fourteenth of September, at Belle Vue, Cusick faced off against the reigning Champion of Scotland, Jim McInally. The bout concluded in a draw, marking the singular occasion Johnny would split the honours with an adversary.

Four weeks later, Johnny was gearing up for his most formidable challenge yet as a featherweight. Johnny King, who held the bantam championship, was not only a top contender for the featherweight title but had also recently secured a notable victory against the legendary Nel Tarleton. The stakes were high, and the spotlight was firmly on Johnny as he prepared to face such a seasoned adversary.

When Jacky Madden, the matchmaker for Belle Vue, came to me with the proposal for Johnny to square off against Johnny King, I hesitated. My gut feeling was that Johnny wasn't quite prepared for an opponent of King's calibre at that moment. However, when I discussed the proposition with Johnny, he was instantly confident, urging me to 'get on with it.'

Given the generous purse on offer, and considering our mutual financial constraints at the time, I found myself swayed to accept the match.

Jacky Bates, who had been training Johnny for quite a while, found himself in a delicate situation, as he also trained King. It was a classic conflict of interest. However, Johnny gracefully addressed the situation, stating that King had the prior claim on Bates's services. He insisted that this arrangement stay intact until after their bout, after which Bates could decide if he wanted to return to Johnny.

There was an adept young man, McCafferty, assisting me in the gym. Collaboratively, we took charge of Johnny's training regimen. I must acknowledge that McCafferty truly stepped up and performed admirably during this period. Moreover, Johnny, fully cognizant of the looming challenge, immersed himself in his preparation, determined to cover all bases and optimize his chances for this pivotal match.

That evening on the twelfth of October, Johnny stepped into the ring in peak condition, a fact that would prove invaluable as the fight unfolded.

Facing a packed audience, the tension was palpable. King, undoubtedly keen on showcasing the devastating right hand that had thwarted many hopefuls aiming for the title, was all in. Johnny, on the other hand, was equally resolute, viewing King as a critical steppingstone in his quest to challenge the reigning champion.

As the bell signalled the commencement of the first round, King instantly took the offensive, pressing forward with a determined aggression. Johnny, however, chose a more strategic approach. He allowed King to dictate the initial pace, focusing on gauging his opponent's style and strategy. This ensured that Johnny stayed clear of any potentially harmful blows that could tilt the bout in King's favour early on.

From the early exchanges, Johnny's superior boxing edge was evident. He masterfully manoeuvred around the ring, using space and footwork to his advantage, frustrating King's efforts to land those body shots.

And while King was busy trying to corner Cusick, Johnny consistently found openings, landing crisp left hands that not only stung King but also ensured that he was amassing a comfortable lead on the scorecards.

As the battle ensued, Johnny seemed in control, orchestrating every sequence with precision. But the unpredictable nature of boxing struck in the fourth round, offering a stark reminder of how swiftly tides can turn.

King, relentless in his pursuit, cornered Johnny, who, in an uncharacteristic lapse of awareness, misjudged his proximity to the ropes. This slight miscalculation was all King needed. Seizing the opportunity, he delivered a devastating right cross, catching Johnny off-guard. The impact was immediate and crushing—Johnny's body crumpled to the canvas, looking every bit the defeated fighter.

The arena, which moments earlier had been buzzing with excitement, fell into a hushed silence, interrupted only by the referee's count.

No one had anticipated this sudden shift in momentum. Yet, to everyone's bewilderment, King seemed hesitant, almost passive. Instead of capitalizing on this golden opportunity to end the bout decisively, he held back. Whether it was respect, overconfidence, or mere miscalculation, no one could say for sure.

But in that brief window, the outcome of the fight hung in the balance, waiting to be tipped.

Johnny, with a fighter's spirit, began to push himself off the canvas, dazed but determined. By the count of six, he was attempting to regain his bearings, his strength returning as the world refocused around him.

King, seeing his opponent vulnerable and yet showing signs of resurgence, experienced a surge of urgency mixed with frustration. The composed, strategic approach he had displayed until this point was overtaken by a frenzied eagerness to clinch victory.

Instead of methodically plotting his next move, he lunged reck-lessly at Johnny, who was still struggling to get onto his feet and regain his stance.

This unbridled aggression might have seemed an instinctive move to finish a weakened opponent, but to many in the crowd, it ap-peared unsporting, even desperate. King's haste might very well have given Johnny the one thing he needed most at that critical juncture: time.

The referee's intervention came as a beacon of hope for Johnny's supporters. With a stern and authoritative demeanour, he stepped between the fighters, holding King at bay. The entire arena seemed to hold its breath, witnessing this pivotal moment. The referee, asserting his role in maintaining the fight's integrity, delivered a sharp rebuke to King, emphasizing the importance of fair play and adherence to the rules.

In the world of boxing, seconds can be the difference between defeat and recovery. As the referee's words echoed through the ring, Johnny used the time to gather himself, shaking off the dizzi-ness and refocusing on the battle at hand.

When the order to resume was given, Johnny, with the instincts of a seasoned fighter, lunged forward, locking onto King in a tight clinch. This wasn't a sign of aggression but a strategic move, giving him time to further regain his composure.

King, now doubly frustrated, tried to break free, but Johnny's grip was unyielding. The referee soon had to intervene once more, prying the fighters apart.

In the intense atmosphere of the ring, every move King made was aggressive, trying to capitalize on his previous success. Johnny, displaying cunning and survival instinct, tactically went down with even the lightest touch, giving himself the maximum time to recover with each referee count.

King, sensing an imminent victory, pressed harder, but Johnny's strategy of elongating the counts, combined with evasive manoeuvres, kept the knockout punch at bay. The round's ending bell chimed just in time, saving Johnny from further onslaught and dashing King's hopes for a quick win.

The fight was far from over.

As the fifth round commenced, Johnny looked visibly shaken, his eyes a touch clouded. While his body moved, it was clear that he was operating more on ingrained instinct than clear strategy.

King pressed his advantage. But, even in his dazed state, Johnny's training and resilience shone through, allowing him to evade any further significant blows from King. The extent of Johnny's disorientation was evident when, during the break, he turned to me and asked if he'd been knocked down.

A remarkable transformation occurred in him as the sixth-round bell rang. The Johnny who stepped out then was the confident fighter we all knew. It was as if the knockdown had never happened. King was now on the receiving end, having to contend with a flurry of punches, both textbook and improvised, as Johnny reasserted his dominance.

With every passing round, Johnny continued to press his advantage, dishing out a relentless assault. By the end, King appeared battered and disoriented, looking more like he had been the one taking those long counts on the canvas rather than Johnny.

The final bell rang, and it was telling when the referee didn't even need to glance at his scorecard before declaring Johnny the victor.

This marked yet another radiant triumph for Johnny, securing him more admirers in the hall that evening than even his eventual title victory would.

Most fighters, faced with such a devastating blow from a boxer renowned as the fiercest puncher in the circuit, would have understandably thrown in the towel. But Johnny, against all odds, stood firm, proving that he possessed both the strategic acumen and the sheer determination to push through the harshest adversities.

Following the match with King, we faced our next formidable challenge.

Allow me to rewind a few months to shed light on why our upcoming adversary marked yet another pinnacle in Johnny's ascent to championship glory.

Back in early 1936, Mr. Hayes was orchestrating fights in Warrington. He came to me with a proposition to match Johnny with the reigning Bantamweight World Champion, the Spanish Baltasar Sangchili, who was then in England. Mr. Hayes had secured Sangchili to spar at his venue against a chosen adversary. He firmly believed that Johnny was the ideal contender, capable of challenging the Champion and giving him a true test of his mettle.

I thus signed contracts for Johnny to face Sangchili in a ten-round bout. However, the Board intervened and vetoed this match, deeming Johnny an unsuitable opponent. This forced the promoter to find an alternative boxer to fill Johnny's shoes. Enter Benny Sharkey, who not only took Johnny's spot but also decisively defeated Sangchili. In fact, the two clashed again a few weeks later in Liverpool, with what I believe yielded a similar outcome.

Understandably, the Board's overreach left both Johnny and me quite aggrieved. So, when the proposition of a clash between Sharkey and Cusick was presented, our enthusiasm was unmistakable. We were both poised to demonstrate to the Board just how misguided their initial decision to bar the matchup with Sangchili had been.

Mr. Bloom, organizing a charity show in Newcastle upon Tyne, reached out to us with an opportunity. Eagerly, I inked contracts for Johnny to square off against Benny Sharkey on 2 November 1936.

It's important to clarify that neither Cusick nor I took Sharkey lightly. With a track record that was truly commendable, Sharkey had faced and triumphed over more champions than most of his contemporaries. Just weeks earlier, he had defeated Johnny King in that very arena. Given Johnny's recent triumph over King, it positioned both fighters on a level playing field.

However, during that period, I genuinely believed that Johnny could stand toe-to-toe with any fighter in his weight class across the country.

The venue was brimming, every seat occupied by eager spectators, all anxiously anticipating which of these two would emerge victorious in the impending clash.

As the bell sounded to commence the first round, Sharkey leaped into action.

Johnny, on the other hand, opted for a more measured approach, taking a moment to assess his opponent. These initial rounds saw Johnny fully engaged, working diligently to evade any significant blows from Sharkey.

Sharkey embodied what Cusick aptly described a 'whirlwind fighter'. Fierce and relentless. Boasting a knockout capability in both fists.

The early stages of the bout showcased a dominant Sharkey, unleashing a barrage of punches from every direction. Meanwhile, Johnny manoeuvred around the ring, dodging and outwitting his formidable adversary.

During the first four rounds, the balance between the two fighters teetered, with neither gaining a clear upper hand. But as the match evolved, Johnny shifted gears. He revealed that his prowess wasn't limited to defence; he was equally formidable on the offensive front.

Adapting swiftly to Sharkey's game plan, Johnny executed a series of dazzling punches, delivering a boxing masterclass that left Sharkey searching for answers.

The battle raged until the eighth round, Johnny steadily amassing a lead on points.

Unfortunately, Sharkey encountered a setback when he injured his foot. Displaying commendable grit, he soldiered on. Yet, his injury left him vulnerable, and he endured a relentless barrage from Johnny for his valiance.

The crowd erupted in applause as the referee declared Johnny the victor.

This triumphant win starkly contrasted the Board's earlier assessment. Johnny had now convincingly beaten the same boxer who had twice defeated Sangchili, a fighter Johnny was once deemed 'unsuitable' to face.

Two weeks later, Johnny found himself in Swansea, facing off against Len Benyon, the distinguished featherweight champion of Wales. Johnny dominated the match with ease.

Post bout, Mr. Moss D'Ong, the evening's referee, remarked to me that Johnny's finesse in the ring evoked memories of Jim Driscoll. It was not the first time Johnny had been paralleled with the iconic, peerless Jim. Coming from a seasoned referee like D'Ong, who had overseen countless top-tier fights in his career, this was undoubtedly a profound compliment.

Merely days later, on 27 November, Johnny found himself filling in for Johnny King at the Tower Circus in Blackpool. He was set to face Harry Edwards, then recognized as the featherweight champion of the Midlands. King had unfortunately sustained an injury during a training session just days prior to the scheduled match, and Johnny stepped into his place at three days' notice.

I had sent Johnny to the weigh-in accompanied by his trainer, planning to join them later that evening, ensuring I'd be there in his corner when the bell rang. To my surprise, upon my arrival at ringside, I was greeted by the sound of the referee declaring Johnny the victor.

The decision was met with a chorus of both cheers and jeers.

Having been delayed by a dense fog on my train journey, I hadn't witnessed the fight, leaving me unsure whether Johnny's victory was justly earned.

Edwards certainly believed he had the upper hand, as he immediately challenged Johnny to a rematch. Johnny, confident as ever, instructed me to arrange it. A few weeks later, in the very same ring, Johnny left no room for doubt, finishing Edwards in just five rounds. It became abundantly clear that facing a well-prepared Johnny was a wholly different challenge than confronting one who had merely stepped in as a last-minute substitute.

Over the next six months, Johnny sustained his winning streak, amassing victory after victory to his already impressive record.

By this stage, Johnny had effectively cleared the path towards a title shot, with only a few top-tier fighters steering clear of him. This evasiveness from the elites meant that finding worthy opponents became a growing challenge. Extended gaps started to emerge between bouts, leading to those headache-inducing periods I've alluded to earlier.

7

THE WEIGHTED DILEMMA

Every attempt to get Johnny into the gym proved fruitless unless a fight was on the horizon. I often tried persuading him to train by implying he had a forthcoming match, even when no adversary was lined up. However, he quickly caught onto this tactic and started insisting on seeing contracts. One can only imagine the condition he'd be in when a real fight did loom, given the irregularity of his training.

Johnny was truly unparalleled in this regard. When not in training, he had an astonishing ability to gain weight. More often than not, he'd find himself needing to shed anywhere from twenty-five to thirty pounds just to return to his fighting form.

It became a recurring pattern, one that could be perilous for any fighter. Yet, Johnny never let it temper his joys outside the ring. He would often quip, 'Just get me past those scales, and I'll handle the fight.' I've frequently realized that preparing him to meet the weight requirement was a greater challenge than prepping him for the bout itself.

The day when he'd reckon with this neglect was looming, though it wasn't upon him just yet.

We now come to Johnny's first appearance in London.

Facing him was Benny Caplan, the reigning Southern Area champion. The match was set on 15 June 1937 at the Harringay Arena.

This bout was the featured undercard for the Farr-Neusel showdown at Harringay, where Tommy Farr triumphantly halted the towering German in just three rounds.

Caplan was in the same league as Tommy Farr. A masterful representation of the classic English boxer, deserving of his spot among the nation's elite. While Johnny had heard tales of Caplan's prowess, he had never witnessed him in the ring. Renowned for his deft use of the left hand, Johnny was considered among the best. Yet for this bout, Johnny thought it prudent to adjust his strategy, diverging slightly from his traditional tactics.

Johnny was keenly aware that when two boxers with similar fighting styles faced off, it often led to a dull match. Eager to make a lasting impression on both the promoter and the audience, he resolved to modify his approach, at least for the initial rounds. If this new strategy didn't bear fruit, he was confident in his ability to switch back to his tried-and-true style.

Facing the largest audience of his career to date, one could easily have expected Johnny to show a hint of trepidation. I'll confess,

I myself felt a wave of nerves, somewhat daunted by this grand stage. Yet Johnny remained unflinchingly composed. To any on-looker, he gave off the impression that performing before such massive crowds was an everyday occurrence for him.

At last, the bell rang, and Johnny burst into action, implementing the strategy he had outlined. He adopted a forward crouch and began hurling punches with both fists, aiming to neutralize Caplan's straight left.

Caplan, likely briefed to anticipate a style mirroring his own from Cusick, seemed taken aback by this aggressive approach. In my view, this surprise allowed Johnny to dominate and set the tone for the entire first round.

Johnny relentlessly pressed on, hooking and delivering punches, securing the round with a distinct advantage. This aggressive approach showcased a side of Johnny I hadn't seen before, and it was captivating to witness him maintain this intensity through-out the bout.

Occasionally, he'd switch gears, adopting a more traditional boxing stance, expertly wielding his left hand. It was as if he wanted to remind his opponent—and perhaps the audience—that he was adept in both styles. But soon after, he'd return to his aggressive, no-holds-barred approach.

This strategy undeniably reaped rewards.

As the rounds progressed, Johnny's lead on points grew increasing-ly evident. Throughout his career, I've often witnessed spectators urging Cusick to step up the pace, but during this match, no one could accuse him of lacking aggression or fervour. Anyone in attendance that night would attest to Johnny's unyielding determination and relentless action in the ring.

The contest ended with Johnny emerging as a clear victor, and the crowd, recognizing his brilliant display of skill and tenacity, showered him with well-deserved applause.

This very Caplan, who was defeated at Johnny's hands, would later turn the tables, setting us back and stalling our pursuit of a title match for nearly two years. The twist in this tale was largely due to Johnny's own doing. I'll narrate that episode in due course.

Taking on a bout as a substitute, Johnny stepped into the ring in place of Benny Lynch in Glasgow. This notable encounter, promoted by Mr. George Dingley, was organized on short notice, and it certainly warrants a mention in our story.

Lynch was matched with KO Morgan from America, an impressive fighter. Just before this bout, Morgan had notably taken down the reigning featherweight champion, Johnny King. Indeed, Morgan had been showcasing his prowess in England for a while and, up to that point, remained undefeated.

Lynch and Morgan were matched at nine stones. However, less than a week before the scheduled bout, Mr. Dingley came to me with a proposal for Johnny to step in for Lynch. Given the lucrative offer, Johnny was quick to say yes. Yet, considering the calibre of our opponent, I felt a twinge of concern given the limited preparation time we had to ready Johnny for such a formidable opponent.

Luckily, Johnny was in fairly good shape at the time. He brushed off any reservations I expressed, leading me to eventually consent to the match. However, I made it clear that our agreement stood only if he could meet the nine-stone weight requirement specified in the contract.

Johnny dove into his training regimen and successfully hit the target weight. With that, I was somewhat assured of his readiness for the match. While the exact date of this contest escapes me, Mr. Dingley informed me it took place in the latter part of 1937.

Regarding the fight itself, the details remain vivid in my memory. So many events transpired in that brief span that evening, making them hard to forget.

The contest took place at Shawfield Park, Glasgow, in the open, and it never ceased raining the whole night. The downpour was so persistent that fighters were carried to the ring on the backs of their teams, in an effort to keep their footwear dry.

As the main event began, a torrential storm further soaked the scene. Those dedicated fans who had endured the earlier fights surely found themselves drenched to the bone, their spirits tested by the weather's onslaught.

Morgan was a master of theatrics, often bringing a flair of show-manship to the ring. However, beneath his playful demeanour lay a fighter of true calibre. His past matches bore testament to this, showing that he was as lethal as they came, making it risky for anyone to underestimate him.

Facing Cusick, Morgan was up against a seasoned pro.

Those familiar with Morgan's style were well aware of his knack for manipulating his opponent, cleverly drawing them into dancing to his tunes in the ring. As Morgan started performing, Johnny swiftly turned the tables, showing him a thing or two about the craft in that opening round.

Clearly perturbed by getting a taste of his own tactics, Morgan responded as Johnny had anticipated: unleashing a flurry of blows from every direction. Yet, Johnny skilfully evaded them, all while delivering sharp left-handed counters.

The bell rang, concluding a round where Johnny clearly asserted himself. Morgan likely felt he was sparring with a phantom.

As the second round unfolded, it became evident to Morgan that his current approach wasn't bearing fruit.

Come the third, Morgan shifted gears, revealing the calibre of a fighter he truly was when he set his mind to it. During this stretch, Johnny was pushed to his limits, deftly navigating to avoid any serious trouble. As the round concluded on a fairly even note, I believed Johnny held a slight edge as they prepared for the fourth, a round that would ultimately decide the bout.

Throughout many of Johnny's initial matches, I observed a consistent pattern: the tougher the adversary, the more exceptional Johnny's performance. It often appeared to me that Johnny exerted just the right amount of effort in his bouts, precisely calibrated to the opponent he faced.

As Morgan ramped up the intensity, Johnny was right there, matching him blow for blow. Morgan's aggressive approach in the onset of this final round left him exposed to a relentless barrage from Cusick.

Midway into the round, Morgan executed a feint and unleashed a ferocious punch that would have surely ended Johnny's night had it landed. However, Johnny deftly evaded the blow and responded with a perfectly timed right cross that left Morgan reeling.

Morgan appeared to lose all composure. He lunged forward, throwing punches haphazardly, not caring about their target.

As fate would have it, one such punch struck Cusick squarely below the belt. Johnny, clearly in pain, dropped to one knee. Without a moment's hesitation, the referee disqualified Morgan on the spot.

At this point, Morgan's temper completely took over.

Just as Johnny was attempting to rise and we were rushing from his corner to help him, Morgan charged him again. The centre of the ring exploded in chaos, with both corners trying desperately to separate the two fighters.

It was a regrettable conclusion to what had promised to be an engaging bout. Nonetheless, Morgan only had himself to fault. Had the match continued its course, I firmly believe Johnny would have clinched a decisive victory.

Up to this point in our partnership, it's noteworthy that Johnny had only been defeated once—that contentious decision handed to Jacky Brown in the bantamweight category.

As a featherweight, Johnny remained undefeated, stringing together a formidable tally of sixty consecutive victories. This streak was a clear indicator of his dominance in the ring, and it showed no signs of ending anytime soon.

After the Morgan fiasco, Johnny continued taking on and defeating challengers from various regions of the country. With this series of victories, my anticipation grew that the authorities would finally grant Johnny the opportunity he deserved: a shot at the reigning champion for the title.

Yet, to our profound dismay, we learned that the Board had decided on yet another eliminator, tasking the top competitors with vying for the chance to face the champion, Johnny McGrory.

The frustration was particularly intense when the selected contenders were announced. Johnny had already encountered and triumphed over the majority of them.

The impact of this announcement was deeply disheartening for us both. We found ourselves confronted with the familiar gauntlet we had already endured in the bantamweight division.

Johnny was selected to face Spider Jim Kelly, the fighter from whom he would eventually claim the title. Their initial encounter on 25 November 1937 in Belfast saw Johnny emerge as the clear victor on points.

Meanwhile, Benny Caplan had emerged victorious in the final of his area, setting the stage for another showdown with Johnny. The stakes were high: the victor would earn the opportunity to challenge the champion for the title fight.

This point in our journey introduced me to a deeper sense of concern than I'd ever known, a level of distress that made all previous challenges and disruptions seem insignificant by comparison.

An excruciatingly four long months elapsed from Johnny's previous bout with Kelly to the day he confronted Caplan again, this encounter coming late in the month of March 1938.

During this period, Johnny Cusick seemingly vanished. Weeks elapsed without any contact, and I had an inkling of his whereabouts. History had shown that when Johnny kept out of sight, it was often a prelude to some unwelcome escapades.

Had I managed to secure some interim matches, things might have gone smoothly, and I spared no effort in this pursuit. Yet, Johnny's renown as a formidable contender preceded him, effectively clearing the field of suitable featherweight opponents.

In desperation, I reached out to potential lightweight adversaries, but understandably, they balked at the proposition. For these lightweights, squaring off against a featherweight of Cusick's calibre presented an all-risk, no-reward scenario—they stood to lose their standing with little to gain, facing someone who could easily upset their rank.

Indeed, Johnny took me on quite the chase before finally settling down to train for this crucial bout. By the time he resolved to show up, he'd often pre-emptively visited the Turkish baths to shed some pounds, in an attempt to convince me he was on track and not undermining his condition with his escapades.

This practice became a frequent routine, a fact that I unfortunately only came to realize too late.

There was a time when I nearly lost all hope of getting Johnny ready for Caplan, and to be honest, the right move would have been to inform the Board and call off the fight. But I clung to the thought that given Johnny's dominant performance in their last encounter, he could not possibly lose this one if I could just get him down to the fighting weight.

I know now how wrong I was.

At this point, I had overestimated his ability to bounce back, and to my dismay, he had taken up drinking more extensively than I had ever imagined.

Speaking frankly, I had been completely duped by this cunning young man. As a result, he made the weight, but he stepped into the ring to face Caplan in a condition where he truly belonged in a hospital bed, not a boxing ring.

The match proceeded, and Caplan secured the decision on points—there's no question he deserved the victory. It might have been the least impressive performance of Johnny's career.

To my surprise, Caplan didn't score a knockout despite Johnny being a mere shadow of his former self, his innate boxing instincts the only thing keeping him upright through the fight. Had Johnny been in proper shape, Caplan, judging by his performance that night, wouldn't have endured beyond six rounds.

I found the entire ordeal so disheartening that I advised him to retire his gloves permanently. It took several weeks before we crossed paths again—by then, Johnny was penniless and managed to charm his way into persuading me to arrange another bout for him.

To my deep regret, I managed to secure him a match on the twenty-eighth of April 1938 with Freddy Miller, Featherweight Champion of the World, in Liverpool.

Tragically, he repeated his previous failings, only to a more dire degree. He arrived to face Miller in a condition that was, if conceivable, even more deplorable than his shape for the bout with Caplan.

Consequently, Miller delivered a knockout in the sixth round, although, in my estimation, he could have concluded the match in the opening round if he had so desired, given Johnny's compromised state.

That night, I parted ways with Cusick, resolved to sever our partnership for good.

8

THE BALLAD OF JOHNNY AND OLIVIA

Johnny met Olivia during one of his despairing moments. On a warm spring morning in late May 1938, he was strolling the city's streets aimlessly, when he stumbled upon a quaint café. It was there he first saw Olivia, a waitress whose simple elegance and serene grace offered a stark contrast to the complex world he knew so well.

Olivia, with her light-brown hair and deep hazel eyes that sparkled with untold stories, moved through the café with a lightness that captivated Johnny. Her voice, melodious and soothing, seemed to sing even in conversation, enveloping him in a tranquillity he hadn't realized he was seeking.

Oblivious to his fame, Olivia approached him with an easy smile and genuine warmth, a refreshing change from the fawning adulation and envy he usually encountered.

'Good morning,' Olivia greeted with a sincere smile. 'What can I get you?'

Johnny, lost in thought, looked up and was immediately captivated by her kindness and warmth. 'Just a coffee please, thanks,' he managed, his voice tinged with a vulnerability he seldom showed. As she walked away, he couldn't help but watching her, entranced by her beauty and simplicity.

With each passing day, the café transformed into Johnny's sanctuary, a haven not just for the coffee, but more so for the moments with Olivia. Their initial exchanges were simple, marked by the casual pleasantries of new acquaintances.

'Nice to see you again, Johnny,' Olivia would greet with a smile, to which Johnny would reply, 'Wouldn't miss it for the world.'

Soon, their conversations deepened, with Olivia opening up about her passions. 'I've always loved music,' she confided one day, her eyes lighting up. 'Singing...it's more than just a dream for me.'

Johnny, leaning in, responded, 'You've got a voice that could turn that dream into reality.'

Their chats became the highlights of his visits, a blossoming connection set against the backdrop of the bustling café. In these moments, Johnny saw reflections of his own hidden desires, yearnings for a life beyond the relentless cycle of training and fighting. Olivia's dreams, vibrant and untamed, echoed the silent longings he had buried under layers of hidden fear.

One day, Johnny mustered the courage to ask Olivia out. She agreed, and their first date was a magical evening filled with laughter and shared dreams. They went to a cosy inn where their laughter filled the air, and every glance between them felt like a shared secret. It was an evening suspended in a kind of timeless magic, where every word, every smile, felt like pieces of a puzzle they were meant to complete together.

Their connection deepened, a bond forged not just in shared laughter, but in the quiet understanding of unvoiced fears and hopes. Johnny listened, truly listened, as Olivia spoke of her aspirations, her words painting pictures of a future so different from the life he knew.

They wandered beneath the starlit sky, their steps echoing along the cobbled streets, fingers intertwined. The world around them faded to a distant murmur.

Even as Johnny's life continued its unpredictable trajectory, his moments with Olivia became an oasis of peace. He treasured every second stolen from his chaotic world, whether wrapped in comfortable silence or lost in the depths of conversation.

Olivia's presence brought a new strength to Johnny's life, a sense of purpose that transcended the physicality of the boxing ring. She was no longer just an escape; she had become an integral part of his existence and the melody to his life's song, filling him with an indescribable sense of strength and determination.

Then, one evening, as they were strolling through the park, Olivia's words fell like crashing thunder. 'I'm moving to London,' she said, her voice a mix of joy and sorrow. 'I've got a singing job.'

Johnny's world teetered on the brink of this revelation. 'London?' he echoed, his voice a hollow rebound of his turmoil. 'But…'

Before completing his words, Olivia hugged him. 'Yes, my love,' she replied, her eyes glistening with unshed tears and a smile that spoke of dreams coming true. 'Aren't you happy for me? You'll visit, support me, won't you?'

The question hung in the air. 'When…When are you leaving?' Johnny asked, his voice barely a whisper.

'Tomorrow morning,' she confessed, her gaze dropping. 'I didn't want to draw out the goodbyes…the pain…' In a moment of raw emotion, she pulled him close, their embrace a fragile bridge between parting and longing.

In the morning, Olivia boarded an early train to London Charing Cross. She arrived around midday and made her way along the narrow lanes of Soho to a dimly lit club that promised the start of a new chapter.

Three days later, still shaken yet resolute, Johnny made a decision. It was time to rewrite his own story. He stood before the door of John Bennett's office.

9

VYING FOR THE TITLE

Following from his match with Freddy Miller, Johnny landed a scaffolding job.

This news brought me some peace; at least his whereabouts and activities were no mystery.

Our silence stretched on until, two months later on twenty-ninth of June 1938, he resurfaced in my office with a resolve to return to the ring. He assured me he had absorbed the lessons of his past and vowed, with earnest, that he wouldn't disappoint me again.

I confess, it gladdened me to find Johnny in such a repentant state, and a part of me yearned to trust that he had recognized the folly of his ways. He made a pledge—if I were willing to take another chance on him, he would demonstrate his undiminished prowess and clinch the title that had long eluded him.

Considering that Johnny was still a mere twenty years of age, I acknowledged the possibility that if his words were genuine, the potential to achieve what he aspired to remained within him. Thus, I resolved to give our partnership another shot.

I required, however, tangible evidence of his dedication before fully committing. I made a conditional agreement: if he engaged in rigorous training immediately and maintained it for three to four weeks, I would regain my trust and seek out matches for him.

On these terms, we embarked on the path toward his comeback.

For the following weeks, I personally oversaw his training, and true to his word, he honoured the promises he had made.

In the interim, Benny Caplan had advanced to a championship bout against Johnny McGrory. However, McGrory couldn't meet the weight requirement on the fight's evening. As a result, the title was left vacant. The Board then designated Caplan and Spider Kelly as the contenders to compete for the now-open title.

Before us stood two fighters vying for a championship, both of whom Cusick had defeated in the past. I was confident in his ability to triumph once more, should the opportunity arise.

George Dingley was orchestrating an open-air boxing event in Dublin, and I petitioned him to slate Cusick against Spider Jim Kelly. Initially, Dingley expressed scepticism, frankly admitting his doubts about Johnny's reliability to even make it to the ring, much less deliver a competitive bout against Kelly, who had remained undefeated since his last encounter with Johnny less than a year prior.

I implored Mr. Dingley with such fervour that I proposed a hefty penalty should Johnny renege on the agreement. Fortune favoured us when Mr. Dingley found himself in need of a credible contender for Kelly, and with the knowledge that Johnny, at least theoretically, was the sole viable candidate at that juncture, he agreed to arrange the match.

This turn of events was a significant opportunity for us. Should Johnny replicate his prior triumph over Kelly, who, as noted, stood on the cusp of a title bout with Caplan, it would place Cusick in the advantageous position of having a previous victory over the new champion, should Kelly emerge victorious.

On a late July evening, with the sun dipping below the brick-roofed houses on the outskirt of Manchester, Johnny returned home earlier than usual. As he stepped through the front door, his mother, her expression a blend of curiosity and warmth, handed him an envelope.

My dear Johnny, the letter began, Olivia's handwriting gracefully traversing the page. Johnny traced the words with his finger, feeling the imprint of her pen. She wrote of her new life with infectious excitement, detailing the bustling nights at the club, her voice among four chosen to enchant the audience nightly, save for Mondays. She mentioned the club's manager, Donny, describing him as a kind soul, a reassuring presence in her new world.

Johnny's heart raced as he flipped the page, skimming past the details of her daily routines, seeking the words that would soothe the ache of her absence. At the end of the letter, her words reached out to him, simple yet profound:

> *Thinking of you. I miss you.*
> *Yours,*
>
> *Olivia xxx.*

For a moment, he stood motionless, the letter clutched in his hand. Then, with a surge of emotion, he bounded up the stairs two steps at a time to his room. There, sitting on the edge of his bed, he unfolded the letter again, immersing himself in each word, each line. He brought it to his face, inhaling deeply, closing his eyes as if to capture her essence. The scent of the paper, mingled with the faint trace of her perfume, transported him momentarily to her side.

He read and reread, letting her words wash over him, a balm to the loneliness that had settled in his heart since her departure. Her words were more than ink on paper; they were a whisper of her spirit, a promise of a bond unbroken by distance.

Johnny's heart sank as he realized, with a pang of disappointment, that Olivia hadn't left an address.

On the fourth of August 1938 in Dublin, Cusick and Kelly faced off once again. Johnny delivered a masterclass in boxing, outmatching Kelly to win by a substantial margin on points.

To add to this Kelly went on from there to defeat Caplan for the title.

Happily, this sequence of events left Johnny with two victories over the new champion.

Johnny's performance, it seemed, had swayed Mr. Dingley's opinion, for he approached me with a proposal for another bout in Dublin against the former champion, at nine stones six pounds. I seized the opportunity without hesitation; should we succeed against McGrory, it would undoubtedly position Johnny as a foremost contender in the Board's eyes for Kelly's title challenge.

Mr. Dingley was experimenting with a novel idea in boxing at the time. He had planned a midnight show at the Theatre Royal in Dublin, an endeavour that, regrettably, did not pay off financially. It became apparent that boxing at such a late hour didn't attract the crowds he had hoped for. Given that there have been no subsequent attempts to replicate this model, it seems that other promoters have taken heed of Mr. Dingley's unfortunate outcome.

When it came time for the weigh-in, we encountered an unforeseen development: McGrory exceeded the agreed-upon weight by seven pounds, which obliged him to pay a penalty.

This positioned Johnny against a formidable obstacle, as he was conceding nearly a stone in weight to an undefeated former featherweight champion. The sheer scale of the challenge seemed to elevate Johnny to new heights of prowess.

As the two boxers squared off in the ring, an air of suspense enveloped the spectators, each acutely aware of the weight discrepancy favouring McGrory. Yet, as the rounds progressed, it became increasingly apparent that Johnny was not just holding his own, but he was orchestrating a masterclass in the sweet science of boxing.

It was as if McGrory had been reduced to a neophyte, trying to read from a playbook that Johnny had rewritten on the fly.

In the aftermath of the fight, amidst the echoing cheers and the adrenaline slowly ebbing from the arena, McGrory extended a hand to Cusick and delivered the ultimate accolade, affirming that Johnny Cusick was, the finest boxer he had ever contended with.

Following Johnny's emphatic triumph, it seemed to solidify his position as the undeniable contender for the featherweight title. The Board, perhaps influenced by this display of boxing acumen, soon made a formal declaration, nominating Cusick as the challenger to face Kelly for the coveted championship.

As we approached our ultimate objective, a single challenge awaited, a challenge I deemed a certainty, as long as Johnny remained steadfast. Kelly, previously defeated, seemed unlikely to reverse his misfortunes against Johnny, who had become his nemesis in the ring.

To maintain Johnny's edge, I frequently suggested that Kelly, now the reigning champion, might present a new challenge, a transformation often ignited by the attainment of such a revered title. Yet convincing a confident fighter like Johnny of a threat I scarcely believed in myself proved difficult.

My nerves were taut during this time, for the unpredictable nature of Cusick left me uncertain if, on any given day, he might jeopardize everything we had worked so tirelessly to achieve. To most, the opportunity to compete for the British title would be a dream, a motivator strong enough to keep any fighter in line. Yet Johnny was an anomaly; he was curiously indifferent to the lure of the championship belt, which was my primary source of anxiety.

Johnny had no ambition at all. His horizon extended no further than the immediate gratification that a few pounds could bring.

In many earnest discussions, I endeavoured to sketch a future rich with prospects, outlining the bounty we could harvest should he clinch the title in his class. On the rare occasions his mood was agreeable, he'd lend an ear and nod along. Yet, more often than not, he'd dismiss my visions with a wry quip—'You preaching again?'—reducing my earnest guidance to the level of tiresome sermons.

During that time, I found myself in a flurry of activity, reaching out to promoters far and wide with the aim of keeping Johnny busy. The spectre of idle time before the title bout loomed, I feared the consequences of too long a wait for a fighter like Johnny.

Fortunately, I managed to match Cusick at Belle Vue with Eugene Peyre, France Featherweight Champion. They stepped into the ring on 6 March 1939.

Cusick was in his element. He outclassed Peyre, securing a KO victory in the seventh round.

The stage set for the title bout against Kelly on 28 June 1939 at Kings Hall in Belfast. A good four months to prepare, Johnny slipped into a steady rhythm of light training. Things progressed smoothly, until, as if on cue about ten days before the contest, turmoil struck.

10

THE CHAMPIONSHIP

On that Friday evening on 16 June 1939, less than two weeks before the fight, I left the gym with an image of Johnny in good spirits, a vision that I cherished as the prelude to our upcoming challenge. However, my arrival at the gym on Saturday afternoon was met with a jarring silence—Johnny was conspicuously absent.

George Johnson, my partner in training Johnny, greeted me with a sombre face. He informed me that Cusick had failed to appear for his morning roadwork, and despite George's diligent attempts to find him, Johnny was seemingly swallowed up by the city, vanished without a trace.

In the fading light of the evening, I finally found Johnny.

He was stumbling out of a club, a bit worse for wear, flanked by a bunch of his drinking buddies. The night had taken its toll, etching exhaustion and recklessness onto their faces. I wasted no time with pleasantries—these were no friends. They were instigators, goading Johnny on in his vulnerable state.

Johnny himself was clearly three sheets to the wind, his words slurring as he defiantly tossing around words about ditching the title fight.

I kept my cool, coaxing him with the promise of a warm bed to get him into the car. He mumbled some agreement and collapsed into the back seat. We were supposed to head home, but I steered us towards the gym instead. By the time we arrived, he didn't care where we were—he was out cold.

With luck on our side, we got Johnny into the gym unnoticed, his state hidden from prying eyes. It being a Saturday evening, the gym was ours alone. We laid him out on the rubbing table, like a fallen fighter between rounds, and there he remained, undisturbed, for a good couple of hours.

After allowing him some time to sleep off the worst of the alcohol, I gently shook Johnny awake. 'Come on, time to rise,' I murmured, handing him a strong cup of coffee. 'This should help clear your head.'

He took the cup with a mumbled thanks, the steam wafting up seeming to cut through the lingering fog in his mind.

Next, I had him take a long soak in a hot bath, followed by a vigorous rub down. Slowly, the haze of the booze lifted from his eyes.

Thinking ahead, I decided to bring him home with me, ensuring he'd stay out of trouble for the night. Tomorrow, we'd have that overdue, heart-to-heart talk.

As the first rays of morning light crept into the room, Johnny stirred awake, his eyes reflecting a deep-seated remorse. Seizing the moment, I confronted him, my voice laden with the weight of pent-up emotions.

'Johnny, we need to talk,' I started, my tone firm yet tinged with concern. 'What happened last night, what's been happening... It can't go on.'

He sat up, rubbing his face, his expression weary. 'I know, I know I messed up—'

'Messed up? Johnny, it's more than that,' I interjected, the frustration evident in my voice. 'You're throwing away everything you've worked for, everything we've worked for. I've watched you fight battles in the ring, but this...' I paused, struggling to keep my emotions in check. 'This battle with the bottle, it's a fight you're losing.'

He looked down, his voice barely audible, a mere whisper. For a moment, he opened his mouth as if to speak, then closed it again, slowly shaking his head.

Seeing this subtle admission, I softened my tone, sensing his vulnerability. 'You've got to make a change, Johnny. And I'm not just talking about your career, but for yourself. Are you willing to do that?'

A heavy silence filled the room before he finally nodded, his resolve finding voice. 'Yes, I am,' he said, his voice stronger now. He lifted his right hand, placing it over his heart in a solemn gesture. 'I promise.'

Ultimately, I sent him home with a stern admonition to be at the gym by afternoon. I gave him a stark warning: fail to appear, and come Monday morning, I'd be on the phone with both the promoter and the Board. He understood the gravity of that threat and the severe repercussions that would follow should I be forced to carry it out.

As the fight approached, Johnny ramped up his training and hit the target weight, giving him a day to rest before we set off for Belfast.

Johnny had to travel by boat, as the promoter would not permit him to fly over. I saw him off with George Johnson, who had helped me train him. I then travelled by air the following morning and arrived in good time to be present at the weigh-in.

Both contenders made weight without issue, setting the stage for what was to unfold as one of the happiest days of my life. To those who witnessed Johnny's spectacular display in the ring that night, it would have been unimaginable that just a fortnight earlier, his conduct nearly derailed this very moment.

The arena was buzzing with anticipation as the fighters stepped into the ring. Johnny's face gleamed with sweat, his resolve unbreakable. This was the fight of his life, a chance to seize the championship that had eluded him for so long.

Our strained silence leading up to the fight faded into the background as he dazzled in the spotlight. He unequivocally demonstrated his dominance, outmanoeuvring Kelly at every turn, culminating in a decisive knockout in the twelfth round.

At last, my dream had become a reality.

Johnny 'Nipper' Cusick had risen to the heights of a British champion, the prestigious Lord Lonsdale Challenge Belt now his to claim.

Reflecting upon our arduous journey, and battles in and out of the ring, it's clear that the most terrifying adversary wasn't in the opposing corner of the ring but Johnny Cusick himself.

Now, at a time when we should have been capitalizing on our victories, Johnny shrugged off the regimen he'd been so strictly following. Even with a host of lucrative offers that could have filled our wallets coming in from every corner of the country, he showed no interest. Johnny only stepped into the ring when his immediate financial needs demanded it.

I explained the folly of his ways, urging him to think ahead—if he could keep himself straight for just a year or so, he could retire comfortably. But it was like talking to the wind. Johnny never thought about the future.

Several weeks post-victory, Mr. John Harding, a promoter, extended an enticing offer for a match in Monte Carlo against Bernard Leroux, France's bantamweight champion. The fight was to take place at Stade Louis II on 5 August 1939 under the auspices of the Marquis of Queensbury. The purse was substantial, and while Johnny agreed, it soon became apparent his sights were set on a paid vacation rather than a bout.

With two weeks to prepare, the duration hardly mattered given Johnny's lax approach to training. We landed in France with three days to spare, yet even after a couple of days of last-minute efforts, Johnny tipped the scales seven pounds over at the weigh-in. Since the event was for charity, M. Harding diplomatically convinced our French opponent to proceed with the fight without enforcing the forfeit.

Bernard Leroux, a capable contender, gave Cusick a rigorous test in the ring. Despite winning by points, Johnny's subpar fitness nearly led to his downfall. Leroux landed him on the canvas with a count of six in the fifth round, spurring Johnny into action. Rallying with everything he had left, Johnny dominated the remainder of the match, nearly finishing Leroux with a knockout in the final moments before the bell intervened, securing Cusick's victory.

If Johnny had been defeated, the fault would've been squarely his own. A well-prepared Johnny could have stopped his opponent earlier in the match.

Mr. Harding likely never forgave Johnny for coming in overweight, and reflecting on it, I'm certain this contributed to Johnny never being featured in London as a champion.

11

THE WAR AND THE DOWNFALL

The war broke out shortly after this contest.

Earlier on, Johnny might've tried to hide from me, to keep his benders under wraps. But as time wore on, he lost even that sense of caution. He'd flaunt his misbehaviour, as if daring me to challenge him. If I did, he'd fire back, 'I won a title for you. What more do you want?'

Things deteriorated rapidly from there.

Offers for fights were turned down one after another because Johnny had made up his mind to step into the ring only when his wallet was empty, often fighting for less than he owed. The debts mounted, and with them, so did our troubles.

He was at this time, twenty-one years old, and due to be drafted into the armed forces. I repeatedly encouraged him to enlist before the inevitable draft, highlighting the advantages of joining the forces as the reigning champion. I reckoned that the discipline of service life might knock some sense into him, and deep down, I knew it might be the only shot of holding on to the title, for if he had to defend it in the state he was in, it wouldn't turn out well at all.

Cusick could be swayed with unsettling ease, yet he was shrewd when it served his interests. He concurred with me on the wisdom of enlisting before the inevitable draft, but each time he edged toward that leap, hesitation clutched him back. It turned into a recurring joke, him showing up with the same worn promise, and us knowing full well it would go unfulfilled.

There came a day when even I couldn't extend Johnny's line of credit any further. His back was against the wall; he had to step into the ring or remain penniless. I discovered, somewhat painfully, that the only method to coax him into a fight was to withhold any financial aid during his times of need. Despite my personal struggles with being tough on him, I realized it was the only way to push him to fend for himself.

The pattern of neglect continued into Johnny's next contest, this time against Frank Parkes from Nottingham—a fighter he had outclassed two years before. But history didn't guarantee discipline. As the weigh-in at Nottingham approached, Johnny tipped the scales with his usual excess weight, three or four pounds too many, resulting in yet another forfeiture to his opponent.

I must concede, with a sense of profound disappointment, that in every contest after winning the championship, Johnny was overweight, a trend that persisted relentlessly until he lost the title.

He defeated Parkes with surprising ease, and it was anyone's guess how he mustered the stamina to box as impressively as he did. Then, with his pockets replenished, he vanished from sight, only reappearing when his finances inevitably dwindled and the need to refill them arose.

At this point, Johnny's reckless behaviour had become an open secret, making promoters hesitant to offer us bouts. Local promoters, in particular, were reluctant to engage with us, and honestly, who could blame them?

We still had a shot at securing matches away from home. Our next fight took us back to Newcastle upon Tyne, where Johnny was set to face Tom Smith of Sunderland on 4 October 1939, a fighter quickly making a name for himself.

Mr. Charlton, the promoter at St. James' Hall in Newcastle, approached me for a bout between Cusick and Smith. Optimistically, I set the match at nine stones five pounds, secretly hoping that Johnny would manage to hit this mark. But deep down, I knew it was futile; even a ten-stone limit wouldn't have made a difference.

With only four days remaining before the bout, I found myself in the unenviable position of having to call Mr. Charlton. I explained, with a heavy heart, that Johnny would be unable to make the weight by the scheduled date. The words felt like an admission of defeat, not just for the upcoming contest but for the discipline we had been striving to maintain.

Mr. Charlton's response was swift and uncompromising: if we reneged on our agreement, he threatened to petition the Board to revoke Cusick's license. Despite my attempts to clarify Johnny's predicament with the scales, Charlton was adamant. His instructions were clear and non-negotiable: Johnny had to show up in Newcastle ready to fight, regardless of his weight.

The firm stance of the promoter was unprecedented in our experience, and it visibly rattled Johnny when I conveyed the gravity of our situation. The looming threat of what might transpire if we defaulted was a stark wake-up call for him.

We reached our destination only to confront the expected: Johnny was three pounds over the limit. This time, the cost of his nonchalance came with multiple penalties.

Smith was declared the victor by points—a decision that seemed unjust to me and nearly everyone in attendance. But it was the outcome Johnny had unwittingly courted through his conduct. Even I had reached the limits of my patience with him.

The situation had escalated to a point where I secretly yearned for an escape from the boxing world entirely.

Covering for Johnny had become a daily ordeal, each new dawn laden with fresh worries. I even began to question his mental state. Some of his actions were, to put it mildly, abnormal.

The silence following our bout with Smith stretched into weeks, until a tempting offer shattered the lull. A match in Liverpool loomed, a high-stakes challenge against Nel Tarleton.

This wasn't just any fight—it was a gambit for the title, an all-or-nothing that demanded Cusick's crown as its ultimate prize.

I wasted no time. I brought the offer to Cusick's attention, eager to see his take. His response was immediate and enthusiastic—he was all in.

I made it crystal clear to Johnny that with his title on the line, I wouldn't stand for any more escapades. The stakes were too high—his future, *our* future, hinged on his commitment. His answer was a solemn vow: he would dedicate himself, train rigorously, and step into that ring in peak condition. The assurance in his voice was new. It carried a weight that was absent before, as if the gravity of the situation finally took hold of him.

My confidence in him swelled. Barring any lapses, Tarleton posed little threat. And Johnny, with a brash certainty that was almost convincing, assured me his grip on the title would not falter against Nel.

Despite his firm resolution, Johnny's next actions surpassed all prior recklessness, discarding the triumphs earned through sweat and toil for the fleeting escape of intoxication. The iron will that had once propelled him through gruelling matches now yielded to an overpowering urge for drink.

As the calendar turned its final page to 1940, the title bout approached ominously on February's horizon. Eager to shake off the indulgences of the holiday season, I thrust Johnny into the rigors of road work, determined that the new year would inaugurate an era of stringent training.

This preparation was not merely routine; it was critical, a foundation upon which his 1 February destiny would be built.

For a fleeting spell, Johnny adhered to our regimen with commendable discipline, and a glimmer of hope sparked within me that he might sustain this diligence.

In an effort to insulate him from temptation, I had whisked him away from familiar haunts to the vigilant guardianship of Mr. Raymond, who was assisting in Johnny's training. Day by day, I shadowed his progress, a silent sentinel, not resting until I witnessed him seated for his evening meal, safely ensconced within the sanctuary of his temporary home.

The calm was deceptively short-lived.

I had slated a press conference for Saturday 21 January afternoon—a mere eleven days before the fight—and upon bidding him good night, I imparted a reminder of our early morning rendezvous. Johnny exuded tranquillity, a facade that betrayed no inkling of the impending tempest that was to unfurl within the hour after our parting words dissolved into the night.

It was Olivia's surprise visit that set off the chain of events.

She had arrived back from London that morning, the city now hushed and strained under the weight of war. Its once bustling streets lay empty, save for the scattered barricades and sandbag fortifications.

Olivia, having sought out Mr. Raymond's address from Johnny's mother, arrived unannounced, driven by a need that overrode all considerations of the long, silent eighteen months that had stretched between them.

The night air was cool as Johnny stepped outside, the world around him fading into a blur at the sight of her. There she stood, a familiar yet distant figure, emerging from the shadows of his longing. Disbelief etched his features, and words escaped him.

Their eyes met, a torrent of emotions swirling in the silence that hung between them. Without a word, they moved closer and hugged. Their embrace was a collision of shared past and uncertain present, a blend of relief and aching nostalgia.

Fingers trembling, they touched each other's faces, tracing the contours as if to affirm the reality of this moment. Each touch a word unspoken, a memory revisited.

That brief encounter outside was all it took. Like a shadow at dusk, Johnny vanished.

I scoured the town tirelessly, my every waking moment consumed by the hunt for Johnny. Scouts fanned out like tendrils, grasping for any shred of his whereabouts, but all efforts seemed futile. Despair was just setting in when the late-night silence was shattered by a phone call. It was past midnight on Monday when the voice on the other end informed me that Johnny had been spotted slipping into Olivia's old, terraced house.

With dawn barely breaking, I made a strategic decision to wait out the night. I couldn't risk another elusive chase in the dark. By 7 a.m., I was on her doorstep, urgency fuelling my movements.

Olivia barely had time to register my arrival before I brushed past her, a man on a mission. I stormed up the stairs to his bedroom where I found him, oblivious to the world, deep in slumber. The morning light crept in, casting a stark contrast on the urgency of our reality against his peaceful repose.

Adrenaline surged as I shook him awake, our confrontation igniting instantly. Words flew, sharp and unyielding, hitting harder than any physical blow could.

'Wake up!' I thundered, my voice slicing through the quiet room like a blade. 'What the hell do you think you're doing?' The words erupted from me, fierce and unbridled, a tumultuous mix of anger and disbelief.

His eyes, heavy with sleep and confusion, fluttered open. 'What the...' His Mancunian accent thick with sleep, he stammered, 'W-what's going on, mate?'

'Going on?' Disbelief and fury laced my words. 'You disappear days before the biggest fight of your life, and you ask what's going on?'

He tried to prop himself up, his movements sluggish. 'I... I just needed some time…'

'Time?' I cut him off. My voice swelled with a rising tide of anger, each word sharper than the last. 'You needed *time*?' I felt my voice climb, not just in volume but in intensity. 'You don't have time! You have commitments, responsibilities!' The last words were almost a roar, an outpouring of pent-up frustration.

His confusion shifted to a defensive anger. 'I can't just live for the ring. There's more to my life than fighting.'

'That's *you*!' I countered. 'That's your life! Your career!' I exclaimed. 'You can't just walk away from everything we've worked for!'

He stood up, a mixture of defiance and confusion in his eyes. 'I just needed some time to clear my head, figure things out with Olivia.'

He never mentioned Olivia to me before. 'Olivia? I echoed, incredulous. 'You risk everything for a...a romance?'

'It's more than that, mate,' Johnny shot back, his voice resolute. 'She means more to me than just a romance.'

I shook my head in disbelief. 'Do you even realize what's at stake here? Your fans, the title, your future...our future?'

Something I said must have struck a nerve, for he leapt out of bed, his eyes wide, mouth opening to speak, but the words never came. The frustration that had been building inside me erupted. My fists flew, driven by a storm of emotions–betrayal, concern, anger–each punch a release of the pent-up fury.

It was then that Olivia burst in, her voice slicing through the heated air. 'Stop it, stop it! It's my fault!' she cried, her words tumbling out in a desperate plea. 'I didn't know.'

Remarkably, Johnny mustered the restraint to not fight back, choosing instead to merely grasp at me, a pillar in my storm. He held firm until my fury subsided into tremors of spent rage.

The sight of my own meltdown seemed to strike a deep chord in Johnny. With a profound look, he suggested we head to the familiar confines of the gym to sort things out. Once there, he recycled his well-worn assurances—he hadn't been overindulging, he insisted. And with a solemnity that suggested a recognition of the gravity of the moment, he offered to press forward with the fight, if that was my desire.

'And Olivia?' I asked, my voice tinged with a mix of confusion and disbelief. My shoulders tensed, my hands outstretched as if grappling with the invisible threads of this revelation.

Johnny shifted, settling on the edge of his seat. His posture collapsed inward, hands veiling his face, a deep breath swelling in his chest before escaping in a measured exhale. 'Olivia has a son, five months old. Named him Johnny,' he said, a wistful smile touching his lips. 'She's getting married…soon, after the war.' His voice was a mere whisper, hands still muffling his words as though to cage them.

He continued, his gaze dropping to the floor. 'Donny, the club manager. She says he's very kind.' Lifting his eyes, he stared blankly at the floodlights overhead. 'They're moving to Scotland, to Edinburgh, away from the war, she said.' A chuckle escaped him, tinged with resignation. 'He's already there, managing his family's' restaurant.' His gaze drifted to the empty ring, lost in thought. 'Olivia's joining him, helping out.'

Then, abruptly, he rose and strode towards the ring, standing in silence as he contemplated the canvas.

'Johnny, you alright?' I called out, jolting him from his reverie.

He turned, his expression unreadable, and walked back. 'Yeah, I'm fine. Let's get on with it.'

That was the last I heard of Olivia. The full story of that lost weekend remained shrouded in mystery, a silent chapter in Johnny's life.

I demanded that he accompany me to the official weights and measures office for an official weigh-in. Resolute in my decision, I was prepared to let him proceed with the bout—if his weight proved satisfactory. At that juncture, my concern for victory or defeat had dwindled, my focus narrowed to the mere fulfilment of obligation, regardless of the outcome.

He agreed, yet nothing could have braced me for the jolt that awaited. As he mounted the scales, a hush fell over us. The inspector read the verdict: ten stones and three-quarters of a pound—fifteen pounds over the requisite weight, with less than seventy-two hours left.

The number echoed in the space, a grim pronouncement of impending disaster.

The moment we stepped out, I was resolute in my decision to inform the Promotor and the Board of Control that the fight was off. Yet, Johnny, in a flurry of pleas, proposed a last-ditch attempt: a visit to the Turkish baths, insisting that the surplus weight was merely water that would dissipate after a few hours of sweating.

His conviction was so earnest that, against my better judgment, I consented. Together, we entered the baths—I was too wary to let him undertake this desperate venture alone.

After six gruelling hours cloistered in the steamy embrace of the Turkish baths on Monday, Johnny re-emerged a diminished man. A subsequent weigh-in revealed a significant shift: seven pounds had evaporated.

Johnny suggested a light meal followed by immediate rest, with intentions to revisit the baths for a second session the following day. Reluctantly, I acceded to his plan, yet I stipulated a condition: he must spend the night at my residence. Resolute in my decision, I was determined to keep him under my watchful eye until we reached Liverpool.

We proceeded with the agreed-upon strategy, and the following morning we returned for his official weigh-in. To our dismay, he tipped the scales at nine stones six pounds. Acknowledging the impossibility of shedding six pounds through conventional means, we had no choice but to make our way back to the Turkish baths.

After enduring another round in the baths, he managed to slim down to nine stones three pounds. This slight turn of events sparked a flicker of hope that he might make the weigh-in after all. Yet, the lingering question remained: could he withstand the rigors of the fight after such a taxing ordeal?

At that moment, my sole focus was on ensuring he made the weight, and I was so driven that I was prepared to push him to the limit, even if it risked his well-being.

Concurrently, I was nearly running myself into the ground. I was with him constantly, and such was my anxiety about letting him out of my sight, I inadvertently lost as much weight as Johnny did.

We repeated the previous evening's post-bath regimen. By Wednesday morning, Johnny was still two and a half pounds overweight. I proposed that perhaps we skip the baths that day and assess how he felt about engaging in some light training in the evening instead.

I kept him inside throughout the day until it was time for the gym session. That night, pity intertwined with my frustration as I watched him struggle for nearly an hour, striving to work up a sweat to no avail.

Johnny proposed that by foregoing food and heading straight to bed, his weight might just dip sufficiently by morning.

Observing his condition, doubts crept in about whether he'd muster the strength to even reach Liverpool, much less endure fifteen three-minute rounds in the ring.

I demanded he eat something light, resolving that if his weight was still an issue in the morning, we would seek a doctor's intervention and attempt to postpone the bout.

Cusick had never been one for hearty meals, but since that chaotic Monday morning when I'd taken charge, his intake had been meagre at best—scarcely enough to sustain even a small cat. We stuck to the plan nonetheless, and after a night of prolonged rest, he looked a little better than he had the previous evening.

We went back to the scales early the next morning, Johnny still a stubborn pound over the limit. He was adamant that the baths would do the trick without the brutal effort of skipping rope in his weakened state. I had to agree. He was too dried out to lose weight any other way.

The steaming rooms of the Turkish baths were our last resort as the hours slipped by. When we emerged and he stepped on the scale, it read exactly nine stones. He had made the weight, but he was on the brink, pale and wobbly. Whether he could fight in this condition was a question hanging heavily in the air, but for the moment, the immediate crisis was averted—he would be allowed to enter the ring.

Upon finally reaching the venue for the weigh-in, we were delayed by snowbound roads.

Nel Tarleton had completed his weigh-in with routine ease. When Johnny stepped up, stripping down for the scales, the room filled with the silent assessments of seasoned onlookers. To those with an eye for the fight game, the evidence was clear—the weight Johnny had shed wasn't from diligent training but rather from desperate measures, and it showed in every line of his depleted frame.

We made our way to the hotel with a sense of urgency, where a hot meal awaited us, thanks to my advance planning. The warmth and sustenance seemed to breathe a bit of life back into Johnny. His pallor waned slightly, his eyes brightened. I ushered him to bed immediately after he ate, instructing him to remain there and rest until I summoned him for our departure to the stadium.

He managed to catch a couple of hours of sleep, which visibly rejuvenated him. When I went to wake him, I asked him how he was feeling. Johnny assured me he felt much better, though I was acutely aware that the backlash from his intense weight loss ordeal was bound to hit soon.

Despite everything, Johnny maintained his belief that victory would be his. However, this time, I found it impossible to share his conviction.

In facing Tarleton, Cusick was up against a true veteran of the ring, and I was sure that Nel would gauge Cusick's compromised state and take full advantage. I was certain Johnny didn't have the stamina to last the fight, but I was wrong—he went the distance. That only underscored my belief that had Johnny been even re-motely fit that night, he would not have lost to Tarleton.

Our secret had been guarded well, as the bookies, unaware of the behind-the-scenes drama, were laying odds of three to one against Tarleton as the match began.

Johnny's resilience was nothing short of astonishing. He showed no outward signs of his recent ordeal in the opening rounds. Yet, from my vantage point at ringside, it was clear that the fatigue was catching up with him—by the fifth round, he was visibly exhausted.

Nel landed a hit in the sixth, a punch that momentarily floored Johnny, triggering a brief count. Under usual circumstances, Johnny would have shrugged off such an impact; the strike lacked the force to cause real damage. True to form, Johnny weathered the remainder of the round with relative ease, untroubled by the blow.

The bout continued, with Johnny largely on the back foot, his fatigue preventing him from pressing the attack and conceding the points lead to Tarleton. However, in a turn of events during the twelfth round, Johnny delivered a solid punch that had Nel teetering until the bell. Despite this momentary upper hand, Johnny's depleted energy forbade him from capitalizing on this fleeting opportunity.

Witnessing the title slip away under such circumstances was utterly heart-wrenching for me. Accepting defeat would have been easier had Johnny been bested by a superior opponent on merit. The final bell tolled, and Tarleton was rightfully declared the victor by points.

Yet a part of me insisted that it wasn't Nel who clinched that contest—it was Johnny Cusick who handed it to him.

Returning home that evening, I was heartbroken, yet I found solace in the remarkable courage displayed by my fighter. Despite the missteps leading up to the bout, he fought with an indefatigable spirit against one of the most skilled opponents to grace the ring.

Johnny was lined up for one last lightweight match before enlisting into the armed services. This would be his final bout in England for the next seven years.

It took place on 22 April 1940 in Belfast, a city that had always favoured Cusick. He had never tasted defeat on Irish soil, and fortune smiled upon him once more. In a closely contested match, Cusick triumphed over points against Al Lyttle, the reigning Irish lightweight champion.

12

CHASING ELUSIVE GLORY

Shortly after his victory in Belfast, Johnny was drafted. Following a brief period stationed in England, he was dispatched to the eastern front in the summer of 1942. It would be four long years before our paths would cross again.

Throughout his time abroad, Johnny's letters were a constant in my life, each envelope heavy with reflections and confessions. The pages within, which I've carefully preserved, are a poignant tapestry of regret for past missteps and squandered chances. They resonate with a solemn vow: a pledge to seize the future with both hands should fate grant him another shot at glory.

Late in 1945, in a letter penned with understated worry, Johnny informed me from India that he was returning to England, mentioning what he called a 'slight touch of malaria.' As time would reveal, his understatement was a quiet battle with a formidable illness.

Johnny's return in March of 1946 was a silent herald of the trib-
ulations he had endured. Yet, it wasn't until November that he
was officially discharged, his prolonged stay in limbo hinting at the
severity of what he had faced.

We were already planning Johnny's return to the ring once he
received his discharge.

I was managing a pub-hotel graced with a spacious backroom,
ripe for transformation. Envisioning a compact training haven, I
petitioned my brewery for consent to repurpose the area into a
gymnasium. Their approval came through, as accommodating as
ever, setting the stage for Johnny's comeback.

In his letters, Cusick had been eager, urging me to lay the ground-
work for his return. He wanted everything primed and ready so that
the moment he shed his military uniform, he could dive straight
into training for the comeback that had become a recurring theme
in our written exchanges.

Resolved to take a more hands-on approach, I decided to personally oversee Johnny's training this time around. In the past,
I had delegated that responsibility, but now I intended to guide
his regimen every step of the way. To create a vibrant training
environment, I coordinated with several young fighters, mostly
amateurs, to spar and train alongside Johnny.

Fresh from his service and essentially residing with me, Johnny
fell into a steady routine: arriving around nine in the morning for
roadwork, spending the day in my company until the afternoon

training session, and then, following a hearty meal, he'd depart in the early evening, around six or seven.

This consistent regimen soon bore fruit. Johnny's form started to echo glimpses of his former glory. While time might have tempered his speed, his technique and ring smarts remained as sharp as ever.

When Johnny was primed for competition, I sought the assistance of Mr. Norman Hurst, a respected sportswriter, to garner interest from promoters. Thanks to Mr. Hurst's efforts, we were introduced to Mr. Reg King, an influential promoter based in Nottingham.

Upon his return to England, Johnny was lighter, easily fitting into the nine-stone category. Yet, I proposed to the promoter a match at nine stones four pounds. The agreement was set, and Johnny was scheduled to face Londoner Billy Marlow on the sixth of January 1947 in Nottingham.

In an ironic twist, Marlow was the one overweight by six pounds. Johnny, displaying sportsmanship, dismissed the weight discrepancy, forgoing any forfeit.

On that night, with Famechon, the French champion, headlining the event, the arena was packed. As Johnny stepped into the ring, the buzzing crowd was dotted with notable sports writers, all present to witness the spectacle.

This stroke of good fortune played out brilliantly for Johnny. His dazzling performance culminated in outmanoeuvring and knocking out Marlow in the seventh round. The next morning's papers were effusive, proclaiming Cusick's triumphant display.

With such prowess, they predicted, he would be vying for his title again in no time.

Given the scarcity of formidable contenders nationwide, the prediction of his imminent rise appeared increasingly certain.

Within a month, the ring called us to Manchester's Belle Vue, a heralded ground for fighters, where we encountered Jimmy Stubbs from Runcorn. Touted as a prospective champion, Stubbs presented not just a challenge but an opportunity for Cusick to reaffirm his place in the boxing hierarchy.

The irony was not lost on me when, for the second time, Johnny's opponent tipped the scales a few ounces over the limit. With a bemused shake of the head, Johnny generously dismissed the weight discrepancy. It seemed almost comical that others now mirrored the very flaw that had so often been Cusick's own stumbling block.

The bout unfolded, and again, Johnny was in his element, winning handily with his signature finesse.

His performance was so impressive that the Belle Vue promoters didn't hesitate. They promptly proposed a match with the reigning lightweight champion, Billy Thomson, to take place at their very next event in the same venue. It was an opportunity that seemed to promise the resurrection of Johnny's career to its former glory.

Within days, contracts were signed, sealing the deal. Victory over Thomson, which seemed well within reach given Johnny's current form, would catapult us into contention for a title shot. And with Johnny now able to make weight at nine stones, both the lightweight and featherweight divisions were viable stages for his impending return to glory.

The preparations for the upcoming contest were intense. Johnny trained with a determination I had not seen in years; he was fully committed to delivering an impressive performance. Yet, as fate would have it, our streak of misfortune was not yet over, and this time, it was not Johnny's fault.

The Board of Control intervened, cancelling the Thomson fight on the pretext that Cusick was too light and the matchup unsuitable. This decision struck me as arbitrary, considering the countless less experienced and capable fighters who had been permitted to challenge champions despite a weight disadvantage.

The press was quick to criticize the Board's authoritarian stance. We exhaustively petitioned for a reversal of their decision, yet to no avail. The Board, ensconced in their authority, remained inflexible, seemingly beyond reproach.

The promoters, facing the challenge of finding new opponents for Thomson and Cusick, saw their bill surge by several hundred pounds. Nevertheless, they upheld the integrity of their commitment. Despite being entitled to adjust the fighters' purses under the circumstances, they opted not to. This act of fairness likely extended to Thomson as well, reflecting a commendable generosity on their part.

Cusick's new opponent was Ben Duffy, a competent fighter, though not as highly regarded as Thomson. Meanwhile, Thomson faced an Irish contender and secured his victory in the eighth round when his opponent retired due to a cut eye.

On 28 April 1947, Johnny triumphed in his match by points, and among the spectators who witnessed Thomson's bout that evening, there was a prevailing belief that if Johnny's fight with Thomson had proceeded, based on the night's performance, Johnny would have emerged the victor.

Next, Cusick was set to face Jean Machterlinck at Belle Vue, in three months on 8 August 1947. The Belgian champion had recently secured two victories against Ronnie Clayton, the featherweight champion of the time.

Johnny, in a departure from his usual approach, was keen to commence his training immediately for the bout with Machterlinck. Agreeing to his enthusiasm, I advised an initial focus on extensive roadwork, putting off the boxing practice until the final fortnight.

I had observed an uncharacteristic quickness to fatigue in his recent fights and attributed it to a lack of sufficient stamina-building exercises. Johnny consented to the plan, and at that moment, I didn't dwell on it any further.

One morning, reality struck harshly when Johnny, returning from his run, collapsed in the gym as I was massaging him down after his bath.

'Johnny!' I cried out, rushing to his side. 'I'm calling the doctor, this looks serious.'

He weakly raised a hand to stop me. 'No, don't... I'll be fine in a few hours,' he insisted, his voice barely above a whisper.

It was then he admitted these episodes had been occurring sporadically since his discharge, although this was the first I'd witnessed.

Perplexed and concerned, I helped him to a seated position. 'This has happened before, hasn't it?' I asked, my eyes searching his.

With a reluctant nod, he admitted, 'Yeah, it's happened a few times since I got out of the hospital in India. But this is the first time you've seen it.'

It dawned on me that the malaria had a tighter grip on him than he had admitted.

Experienced in self-care, Johnny proposed immediate rest. I urged him to stay at my place, driven by worry and a need to understand the toll this cunning illness was taking. It became clear his urgency to train was partly an effort to combat the disease.

That night, I made sure he was comfortably settled in bed, with hot water bottles and a heap of blankets. By morning, to my immense relief, he seemed rejuvenated, raring to get back to training.

But I held firm. 'No training today, Johnny. You need more rest.' I insisted, determined to see him fully recover.

He protested lightly, but eventually conceded, and by the following morning, he appeared to have shaken off the worst of the illness.

From that point forward, I couldn't shake a persistent unease regarding his condition, haunted by the thought of what might happen if he succumbed to a relapse mid-fight, with little to no warning, as he had intimated these episodes struck abruptly.

Johnny remained in good health up until the fight, showing no further symptoms. In peak condition and brimming with confidence, he asserted that defeating Machterlinck would undoubtedly position him for a title challenge.

The fight's outcome dealt us another unfair hand when referee Mr. Teddy Walthem awarded the victory to Machterlinck, a decision that contradicted the consensus of everyone present, including the press. Not a single fight report concurred with the referee's call.

This contentious decision significantly influenced my resolve to convince Johnny to hang up his gloves. From the onset, I held the belief that Cusick's defeats were self-inflicted, stemming from misconduct and poor conditioning. However, in the case of this verdict, I stood corrected, though solely regarding the outcome. The question of how Mr. Walthem came to his decision that night has often perplexed me.

Recovering from our latest defeat, I sat down with Johnny for a candid discussion, emphasizing the risks of continuing his boxing career given his current health. At his behest, we concurred that he would step into the ring one last time. The outcome of this bout would be decisive, sealing his fate in the sport—whether to hang up his gloves or fight on.

The harsh reality of the business is that promoters are drawn to winners, but Belle Vue, perhaps as a gesture to atone for the rough hand dealt to Johnny in his fight with Machterlinck, extended another offer. They proposed a bout on their upcoming bill against Frankie Williams from Liverpool.

The passage of time had brought many challenges, but it all culminated on the seventh of November 1947. That day marked an era's end as Cusick stepped into the ring for what would be his final bout under my management.

Williams entered the ring with a clear strategy, coached to leverage his strength by focusing on landing powerful right-hands on Cusick. In the first round, he pursued this plan single-mindedly, throwing right after right in an attempt to connect with a decisive blow. Despite his persistence, Williams found himself unable to land these intended punches as Johnny, the more skilled boxer, evaded the onslaught. The disparity in boxing technique was evident from the outset—Williams relying on force and Cusick on finesse.

Johnny, adept at avoiding Williams' aggressive, albeit uncoordinated, attacks, seemed to be in a favourable position. With Williams exerting himself in futile attempts to land punches, it appeared likely that Johnny could simply bide his time, letting Williams tire from his own exertions. Once Williams' energy waned from the ineffectual barrages, Johnny could capitalize on this and steer the bout towards a straightforward victory.

Cusick's strategic prowess paid off when he anticipated Williams' repetitive approach and delivered a powerful right hand that nearly finished the bout, sending Williams to the mat for a count of nine.

Poised to capitalize on this advantage, Johnny followed up with a left hook aimed to seal the victory. However, the fight's dynamics drastically shifted when Williams inadvertently absorbed the blow with his head, resulting in a fractured hand for Johnny.

This injury not only thwarted Cusick's immediate plans to end the fight but also imposed a severe disadvantage for the remainder of the match.

As the bell signalled the end of the round, a sense of urgency overtook me—I was poised to signal the referee, ready to put an end to the match. Yet, Johnny, with that undying fighter's glint in his eyes, brushed aside the notion. Despite the pain etched across his features, he insisted on persevering, clinging to the belief that just one more well-placed right hand could turn the tide in his favour.

As the rounds unfurled, the third and then the fourth, time seemed to stretch and compress in the thick of the fight. In the fleeting respite of the fourth interval, my voice was a constant, a drumbeat of concern, urging Johnny to consider his well-being over the win. Yet, he was unyielding, his confidence unshaken—he believed, with the certainty of a seasoned warrior, that victory was still within reach, that he only needed one more chance to strike true.

My conscience weighs heavy with the burden of that decision.

I knew more than anyone the grim reality of Johnny's condition: his left hand rendered a source of agony rather than strength. I stood at the precipice of a crucial choice as the bell heralded the fifth round. With the weight of responsibility anchoring my words, I made it clear to him: 'Johnny, this is it. If you can't put an end to this in the next three minutes, I'm throwing in the towel.'

The unsaid truth between us was that this might be the end of the road, one way or another.

Williams, now keenly aware of Cusick's handicap, regained his composure from the earlier hit and resumed his assault with renewed vigour. His right hands, once flailing ineffectively, found their mark when one thunderous blow landed squarely on Johnny's chin.

The world must have spun for Johnny as he crumbled, his knees kissing the canvas.

In a daze, he latched onto Williams' legs. His fighter's instinct driving him to stand, to cling to the fight, his grip as desperate as his situation.

The referee's voice cut through the commotion, commanding Cusick to release his hold, but whether Cusick couldn't hear or simply couldn't process the command amidst his daze, he maintained his desperate grip.

With decisive action, the referee intervened, prying the fighters apart with authoritative hands. He pointed Cusick towards his corner, a gesture that served as the silent prologue to the inevitable verdict about to be declared.

The referee's actions extended beyond the ring.

In a move that compounded our dismay, he summoned Johnny before the Board, where, notwithstanding the doctor's immediate certification of Johnny's fractured hand, a ten-pound fine was imposed for his supposed infraction.

The fine felt like a punitive afterthought, a bureaucratic twist of the knife in an already painful defeat. The closing events crystallized my resolve: it was time for Johnny to hang up his gloves. His lengthy recovery—twenty weeks immobilized by plaster—provided ample opportunity for heart-to-heart discussions.

Johnny's fighting spirit remained unquelled, but it was no longer the thrill of the sport that fuelled his desire to fight; it was the pressing need for financial stability, a means to transition into a livelihood less punishing and more predictable. The harsh reality that boxing was a precarious foundation for his future was a pill just as bitter as any defeat he had faced in the ring.

Finally, I prevailed, but it took laying down an ultimatum: if Cusick chose to fight on, he would have to do so without me in his corner.

I made it clear that my conscience could no longer bear the weight of his well-being in such a hazardous pursuit. This, perhaps, was the hardest blow I had to deliver—severing the professional ties that bound us, not out of anger or disappointment, but out of a profound sense of care and duty to a fighter who had already given more than the ring had ever returned to him.

So came the fall of Johnny 'Nipper' Cusick's tumultuous yet dazzling career. He possessed all the makings of a boxing legend except the one critical component: passion.

In the end, amid the echoes of a crowd's roar and the whisper of gloves on canvas, his truest battles were waged in the solitude of his own soul, where the hardest punches were thrown, and it was there he met his match.

EPILOGUE

Several months following the match with Williams, Johnny took a job as a coach at the local gym in Hulme where he remained for about a year before retiring completely from the boxing world in the spring of 1949.

He never cut ties with Olivia. Each Christmas, even amidst the chaos of war and his deployment in India, he made it a point to send her a card.

In the summer of 1948, he travelled to Edinburgh. There, standing at the doorstep of Donny's restaurant, he glimpsed Olivia amidst the bustle of serving customers. The sight gripped his heart, evoking a poignant memory of their first encounter in that Manchester café.

That visit, charged with unspoken memories, might have been the last flicker of their shared past. When Johnny returned to Edinburgh again, the atmosphere was heavy, emotionally strained. His reliance on the bottle had grown, casting a sombre shadow across the household. Little Johnny, now growing in the shadow of his namesake, was often spooked by him. Olivia, torn between old affection and her present life, felt the tension gnawing at her relationship with Donny. It reached a point where she found herself compelled to ask Johnny to leave.

Johnny sought redemption in rehab, where he gradually reined in his battle with alcohol. He found a simple yet fulfilling rhythm in life, engaging in various odd jobs and occasionally, albeit rarely, coaching when asked for help by an old friend. He kept contact with John Bennett until his untimely death a few years later. The loss of John, who succumbed to a heart attack at fifty-eight, marked the end of an era for Johnny.

Johnny remained unmarried. His life, a mosaic of triumphs, struggles, and quiet redemption, came to a peaceful close at the age of seventy-two. On 1 March 1990, he passed away due to natural causes, leaving behind … a vague memory.

In the hush that settles over an empty life where shadows of past glory dance in the corners, Johnny 'Nipper' Cusick's story, and perhaps the story of many who tread a lonely path for greatness, was a turbulent odyssey of the relentless pursuit for a cause that fill the void within.

Perhaps, from his early days, Johnny embraced the comfort of doing what he knew best, ensuring just enough for the simple pleasures of fish and chips and few drinks. Ambition, that elusive siren, never called loudly enough to lure him from the comfort of the known and the safe.

Perhaps he never encountered the right moment to step beyond those bounds, or maybe, in a life quietly resigned to the rhythm of the familiar, he never felt the urge to seek it out.

I would be delighted to hear from you.

Please send your thoughts and questions to
philip.amortila@gmail.com

Wishing you all the best,

Philip

SELECTED BIBLIOGRAPHY

Alchetron. *Johnny Cusick, https://boxrec.com/en/proboxer/55749. Dec 16, 2022*

Bearshaw, Brian. *Champ Who Fought for Fish and Chips, The Bloodtub Days, Manchester Evening News, Weekend Magazine, 21 February 1970*

Bennett, John. *Johnny Cusick, Ex. Featherweight Champion of Great Britain and the British Empire, 1951 - Unpublished Manuscript*

BoxRec. *Boxing Record for Johnny Cusick, https://boxrec.com/en/proboxer/55749*

Davison, Malcolm. *Boxing at Monte Carlo, https://www.cuckfieldconnections.org.uk/post/1939-boxing-at-monte-carlo, 7 August 1939*

Daily Sketch. *Cusick signs with Brown, 28 May 1936*

Dudayev, Shahan. *The Art of the Sweet Science: Boxing Training for the Body and Mind, 27 May 2021*

Famous Fix. *Johnny Cusick, https://www.famousfix.com/list/boxers-from-manchester.*

Magowan, Jack. *Boxing: Era when world titles counted, 7 February 2004 https://www.belfasttelegraph.co.uk/news/boxing-era-when-world-titles-counted/28198481.html*

O'Riordan, Turlough. *Dictionary of Irish Biography, Jimmy (Spider) Kelly, https://www.dib.ie/biography/kelly-billy-spider-a9834*

Templeton, Miles. *The other breaks in boxing history, https://boxing-newsonline.net/the-other-breaks-in-boxing-history/, 7 April 2020*

The Guardian. *3 August 1934, Boxer who bit a man's ear, https://www.theguardian.com/century/1930-1939/Story/0,,126978,00.html*

Wikipedia. *Jackie Brown, https://en.wikipedia.org/wiki/Jackie_Brown_(English_boxer)*

_____. *Johnny Cusick, Wikipedia, https://en.wikipedia.org/wiki/Johnny_Cusick*

_____. *Johnny King, Wikipedia, https://en.wikipedia.org/wiki/Johnny_King_(boxer)*

Printed in Great Britain
by Amazon